Praise for Monkey Poet

WINNER! Editors' Award, Edfringe 2014
THREE WEEKS

"Sublime genius, full of moments to treasure. We were in the hands of a master. A cracker of a show"
BROADWAY BABY

"Working-Class Socialism. A throwback to the 80's and that's no insult."
THE SCOTSMAN

"A tour-de-force performance from a man that's a poet, comic and actor. If he was a musician he'd be Billy Bragg."
VENUE MAGAZINE

"Blunt, comically dark and thoroughly entertaining."
DAILY INFO

"Beneath his unabashedly raunchy exterior beats a heart in search of common human decency."
NUVO, INDIANAPOLIS

"Topical, original, and delivered with style. Not one for the easily offended but this audience were in stitches."
THREE WEEKS

"Funny, filthy, furious. Dominates the stage."
JERSEY EVENING POST

TRiBE!

Collective Monkey Poet
(performances 2007-2014)

Burning Eye

TRiBE!

CONTENTS

INTRODUCTION

I've been writing poetry from ever since I can remember, though not continually, a decade off here and there. My first piece of note was at a primary school trip to Burwardsley near Chester. Inspired by the surrounding woodland I wrote a piece called *The Tangling Tree*, about a homicidal Larch or Beech or Oak or whatever, which I was surprisingly commended for and duly instructed to write down, along with fellow classmate Joanne Hollinrake's poem, in Burwardsley's memory book commemorating the two nights we had spent there.

How old I was I don't know, but it was at that age when boys show girls their willies. If memory serves, I'm sure someone got caught doing just that. I wonder if the memory book is still there, gathering dust in the centre's cellar with a thousand other dusty school-trip memory books. I still remember a couple of lines from the poem, "A woman wakes up in bed, to find her husband without a head..." It had also been inspired by the film *The Abominable Dr Phibes* starring the legendary Vincent Price which had left a profound mark, like a gash, on my fragile brain. I didn't sleep much after seeing that film.

Fast forward twenty years and I'm in Manchester. In a bar between bands, a guy ambles up and recites a poem (not that I knew then but it was the soon-to-be-legendary Mike Garry). My first thought was, "Can you do that? Is it allowed?" My second thought, "I can do that!" Years later, chatting to Mike, we commented on the fact that that's how people seem to get into performance poetry. First exposure to it, then trying your hand.

I've had people telling me I inspired them (as did I that night to Mike). And they've said to me, the first instant is a shock, the "Oh, my word, this is brilliant!" moment, quickly followed by, "I'm pretty sure I can do better than that."

This is because poetry is the most accessible of the written art forms to actually do, like painting is to sculpture, a poem is to a novel. You don't need punctuation, grammar, character arcs or a narrative (though you can use all of these things),.You can interchange numbers for words like "2" for "to" and so on, whatever you want, and because of that everyone, from every background and level of education, can do it and each voice is unique. I find it easier to critique a performance over a poem. A poem is personal and who the hell am I or anyone to comment on it.

I performed my first piece of poetry at a night called Manky Poets at the Chorlton Library in Manchester, in September 2004. My brother's girlfriend (now wife) had told me about the night and dragged me (willingly) along. It's still running and happens on the third Friday of every month. Copland Smith runs the night and is a lovely fella, there's something of the gracefully-ageing-hippy-folkster about him and this comes across in the relaxed easy atmosphere of the night. In the first half he goes round the room and everyone has a chance to read, if the numbers are low he'll go round the room again so you read twice. Then after a quick fag break, the headline act will appear. The pieces were a gentle mix of nature poetry, observations, relationships and so on. I got up and read my piece, *That Fucking Fucker's Son*, about me shooting an eight month old baby.

The headline act was Tony Walsh and he told me that another night, Per-Verse run by Conor Aylward, would be perfect for my stuff. Manchester at that time was a melting pot of poetry manna. Not only the people already mentioned but Chloe Poems, John G Hall, Dike Omeje, Steph Pike, Segun Lee-French, Shirley May, Ben Mellor, Jackie Hagan and so on. I did my first 10 minute spot on the 9th June 2005, at the Contact Theatre. How do I remember that date? It was the date an incredible poet I'd seen support the incredible band Half-Man Half-Biscuit at the Manchester Academy died, Hovis Presley. I opened the paper backstage and read in shock about his death. I recited the only poem of his I could remember on stage in heartfelt eulogy: "*I once knew a girl called Lola or Layla, she said make me breathless, so I hid her inhaler.*"

September that year I was back at Manky's for my first headline spot. This time *Fucking Fucker* and *Religious Nuts*

("*Fuck the Moslems, fuck the Jews, fuck the Christians and fuck the Hindus...*") played better. In the audience was Albert Radcliffe, Canon Emeritus for Manchester Cathedral who pronounced the work as "having a very moral dimension". I was cock-a-hoop. I had my first usable quote! I starting performing at music festivals like the Big Chill (my first pay packet from poetry, a hundred pounds. I tell ya that cheque was the best I ever cashed!) and a gig as part of the BLUE3 festival of new arty work at the Royal Exchange in Manchester.

But "how do you make money, real money from poetry?" I thought, "How do you make a living?" A question that was put to me in 2008 by a young Kate Tempest. A question answered for me by Jem Rolls. My then girlfriend Lucia Cox (now a respected theatre director) booked Jem at a short lived night I was hosting. I asked him that question rather drunkenly after the gig, it was my first chance to talk with a living this-is-my-livelihood-and-nothing-else-poet "How, Jem, how?"

"Ah," he replied sagely, "I never made any money till I went to Canada."

PER's FREE FRINGE 2012

MONKEY POETS "POTTY MOUTH"

4-25 august

EXC. 14TH

5.10PM

THE BANSHEE LABYRINTH

PHOTO: www.bloomingphotography.com

PART ONE
Stand Up Monkey Poet!
First performed at The London Fringe, Ontario, 2007.
Winner: Producer's Pick & Best in Venue, London Ontario; Best in Venue, Indianapolis; Best Poet & Technicians Choice Award, San Francisco.

That Fuckin' Fucker's Son

"It was me!" I cried, "I held the gun
that shot that fucking fucker's son,
though the kid wasn't even one,
it was me that held the gun."

You see that fucking fucker,
he angered me,
the way he went on in the factory.
So I went home and got my gun
and shot that fucking fucker's son.

Well, most people were livid,
the newspapers went spare,
some talked of mobs and lynching,
and stringing me in the air.
Because it was me you see that held the gun
that shot that fucking fucker's son,
I know it's not very fair.
But you see,
his Daddy really angered me.

The papers screamed out for Justice,
and tried to invoke God's will.
I said, "Hold on half a second,
it was God that made me kill."
I said, "Don't you remember David?
him of Goliath fame?
Well, years after that
David made an error,
and down in anger God came.

And he took from Dave his youngest son,
his youngest son, not even one,
and the Lord did it in His Own Name."

So, I said,
"Following His example, I set out and made my own,
and shot that fucking fucker's son,
a sin for which I can never atone."

But,
people use God to justify anything.

Filibrium

I live in Withington, With-ing-ton,
every name has a story to tell,
and I know part of this one,
so tell, I well *

Ing-Ton means Mining Town,
like Winnington or Warrington,
mining-Town of Winn, Mining-Town of Warr
Knutsford is where King Canute first crossed his ford.

All this dates back to earlier days,
when men were Men, the women, Women,
and the cattle grazed on the green fields of Withington.
far back to an earlier time of Pagan Ritual and Celtic rhyme,
before Lindisfarne's Gospels spread the Word,
before isolated villages became one herd,
one breed,
one creed.
Way before the Churches eventually disagreed,
before the Angles came onto the scene,
before an United Kingdom was even a dream.

Now steeped in this knowledge and history
I have but one question to give...

Who the hell was With?

*Ignore that rhyme!

My Learning Diffi culty

Spastics – they're easily ignored.
Are they having fun?
Are they fucking bored?
I don't know.
Nor do I about their lives.
You see every time one walks, shuffles or
Wheels themselves past
I avert my eyes.
Why?

Because this feeling wells up inside of me,
A feeling of helplessness and tragedy;
Of life's twisted comedy;
Of grateful, that it's them and not me;
Of love given unconditionally;
Of the courage of some families;
Of bravery in the face of adversity;
And of their frustration –
At unwanted sympathy.

I get a lump in the throat, the swelling of a tear,
Maybe even a hint of fear.
I just wish that they were "Right."
I can't make them, try as I might,
So I pen this useless turd,
But when I do die, God,
You and I will have words.

Intro to After Tennyson

It wasn't just the idea of long-term poverty
that attracted me to a career in Poetry,
it was reportage, journalism, holding a mirror to Society,
like Homer did in the Odyssey,
or Tennyson, who span it politically,
you see,
Into the Valley of Death rode the six-hundred,
cannons to the left of them, cannons to the right of them,
turned a stupid bloody butchery
into Romantic Tragedy.

Which is why this is called…

After Tennyson

Into the valley Baghdad dropped six hundred bombs,
falling faster than gravity
because George had promised liberty,

of the people's legs, just below the knee*

* It was quite hard to watch the footage of the population of Iraq turning out for their long promised free elections when one noted how many had lost legs. Freedom isn't free, to quote an American bath towel but surely that price isn't right.

Fucking Retard

I looked up in the Dictionary of Political Correctness
the other day,
certain phrases that on the playground we used to say,
Fucking Retard is a good example of one such,

but things change…

Nowadays it's only used
To describe George Bush

Crash

Man the lifeboat,
Man the pumps,
Keep the house afloat before another one jumps.
There's debt in the kitchen, debt in the hall,
I've got Debt from my ceiling,
To my laminated floors.

Debt is everywhere,
And the strange thing is no fucker cares.
I've got a slate at the pub, the car's on tic
I'm HP'd* to the hilt,
What a fucking prick!
The petrol's gone up,
So has the food,
And if they mess with the interest,
I'm royally screwed.

There's one solution
And it's for the best.
Flog the house
And buy a bottle of meths.

HP: Hire Purchase. A simple method employed by companies to extract more for goods, generally targeting the poor.

Television

On your shimmering silver screen,
where the fantasy stops the clarity,
and your brutality slo-mo's the insanity,
we gaze upon, like headlight-locked deer,
we're all trapped in glare-mode, can't help but to stare,
though there's nothing really there,
except for your hallucinating light.

You provide
my friends and family
with the only soap-sudded greasy reality
we'll ever need.
Pauses are pregnant with aborted conversations
that never had the chance to begin.
Forget Big Brother watching you,
we're all too busy watching him.
The de-generation game is on every single night,
and keeps silent those who would strike
with your hypnotising, hallucinating light.

I mean,
how can I start to fight
your thousand channels of ultra-shite
beamed into my home
every single fucking night.

The Sacred Art of Self Abuse

I have my dick in my hand, a tab in my mouth,
there's porn on the telly, and I'm sat on the couch.

Is this the real me?

Or some seedy little aspect that didn't previously exist?
I shall go and ask my analyst
because she understands the needs of a man,
the reasons, the wherefores, where morals should stand.

This all started when I began school,
they said I'd go blind,
but sod it,
shades were so cool.

Love Stains

I fall in love so easily,
it's almost like I slip.
If the girl behind the counter should smile,
then that's it, I'm smit.

My friend said once, *"Matt, Love is like stepping in shit –*
It's not the initial step that counts, it's how you deal with it."

I've got Love trodden in my carpets.

The Boy with his Finger in the Dyke

I spent a night with this woman,
it was fantastic, it was sublime
she'd been a lap dancer for ten years,
(so she hadn't seen the best side of men.)
Her tight and taut body moved with a rhyme
and a rhythm all her own,
we gulped at each other greedily all night
and in the morning, dazed and sated,
I staggered home.

Then…
My calls unanswered,
my flowery texts un-replied,
my messages increasingly desperate
as I forgot all about my pride.

And two whole months later
we bumped into each other in the pub,
the atmosphere – really cold
and her eyes held no lies as the truth she told,
"I'm sorry, I just don't fancy you," she said,
"you're not the one I wish to kiss,
occasionally I like a bit of cock,
when I'm out on the piss."

And there's not much you can actually say to that.

"I'm sorry to have to tell you this," she said,
"but this is where it ends.
Can we not just sit and chat?
Can we not try to be friends?"

I said, "Of course we can, of course we can,
Cheers, Ta!"
So, I pulled her up a chair at the table,
and bought her a treble-vodka at the bar.

My Cancer Karma

Seeing the cancer suck the life out of your body
leaving only the husk of a stranger
is enough for me to postpone these hospital visits.
An act of pure cowardice?
Maybe.

The years pass, but time takes you no further from my thoughts.
Coincidence reunites us twice more.

Firstly, cancer has snuck in me,
leaving me in a room rank with the odour of sterility.

And secondly, no one disturbs my door.

People try to steer clear of cancer,
though its popularity
is truly beginning to soar.

Crap Analogy

Life is like Football.
You're beaten by the Hand of God,
the Law of Sod, and Chelsea's mob,
and age and injury retire us all prematurely.

But you can have fun whilst you're on that pitch,
please make the most of your ninety minutes.

The Rackenach

With her scabby lips and crusted eye,
and dewy maw between her thighs,
the Rackenach comes out to play.
Out from the mountains that hide her away,
down through twisted woods to the sleepy village,
she crosses the twin streams called rape and pillage,
clambering up the muddy sides
to find a child to make Three-Screams Pie.*

The Rackenach walks from door to door;
the Rackenach, pus leaks from her sores;
the Rackenach, her day has come;
this Rackenach will eat your Mum!

The creature walked down dirty lanes,
pressing hairy nostrils to the window panes,
grumbling on, nursing her swellings,
as she peered in to the rustic dwellings.
Keenly listening for a Child's soft sigh,
the Rackenach wants her Three-Screams Pie.

Her tongue gets wet, she licks her lips.
The first scream comes when the child is dipped
into the boiling salty sauce.
The second scream comes when she stabs her fork.
Lifting the child to her broken mouth,
the third scream comes when the teeth SNAP down!
Crunched and munched into tiny bits,
gargled down her throat it slips
into the creatures fiery belly,
where bones transform to liquid jelly.

The child now reduced to a slimy goo.
What was once pure,
has become Rackenach pooh!

* *Bizarre Magazine reliably informs me that Three-Screams Pie is a Chinese Dish that utilises live baby mice. Screams are elicited as described.*

Tommy

Little Tommy Tucker,
he's a right little fucker,
he's never been square in the head.
He took home Mrs Jones from the Provident Loans
and there's a very real fear that she's dead.

When he was small, about 12 inches tall,
he had a fight with the cat to the death.
The Cat went "RAWR!"
He went "HAH!"
And the Cat keeled over from his breath.

He saw Mrs Stokes, a lonely old goat,
she's famous for being *mutt'n Geoff*.
He ate her bladder with gall,
kidney stone and all,
and when they buried her
there wasn't much left.

Little Tommy Tucker,
never much of a looker,
said it all happened cos he had no love.
Yet sent straight to Hell,
like all ne'er do well's,
The Devil now wears him
like a glove.

Mary

Mary Whitehouse is dead,
There's no one to carry the flame,
Now I can see Schoolgirls pee
On the chests of hairy Danes.

Mary Whitehouse is dead,
There's no one to carry the crusade.
The pawns are in porn,
The innocent forlorn,
And you never know who has AIDS

Mary Whitehouse is dead,
Nothing'll be the same,
Advertising boards advertise whores,
And who can we really blame?

Mary Whitehouse is dead,
And maybe it's for the best,
Eighty percent of the internet now
Is driven along by breasts.

Mary Whitehouse is dead,
And I don't want to make her a saint,
I've done things that'd curl her toes
Or even make her faint.

She opposed the sexual drive
On the cinema and on the telly.
But today if she'd been alive,
She'd have fire in her belly.

Fire enough to just say, *"No!*
You've taken things too far,
Yes, I'm an old stick in the mud,
But you don't need tits to sell cars."

The Book of Profits
Ledger 4: Folio 12

I was born
into the age
of the Accountant,
not Accountability.

The Pound cried havoc;
The Dollar prowled;
The Yen considered Seppuku.

Romanticism died forlorn,
strangled in bureaucratic rigid trend.
The seeds were sown for a new era

The Age of Legislation.

Cities were reborn to encourage new ideals.
The Moon and Planets were conquered.

Man took his Great Message
to the stars...

"You can buy it cheaper from here."

A worrying Case of Cunnilingus

Tony?
Why did you kiss Bush?
It didn't make you look tough.
Like a Schoolgirl on a street corner,
always waiting for the local hero to walk by,
stop and turn, maybe catch your eye,
even scratch your d e

                        e

               p

                 e

                s

                t

                  l

                  i

                  t

                  t

                  l

                  e

                    itch.

But Tony,

             This wasn't like that.

                    You were his fucking bitch.

Religous Nuts

fuck the moslems and fuck the jews,
fuck the christians and fuck the hindus,
fuck the buddists, the papists,
the trappists, and the pap
that makes them think they're special!
that they shine in the crap
to be the favoured ones in god's vision,
in allah's mission,
enlightened by buddha,
championed by christ,
made masters by mohammed,

i think of them all as i do pubic lice

parasites
who'll never sever the ties that give them their power
or end the lies that corrupt guides
meant for peace and harmony.

just look at our leaders...
tony and george,
its good to know that you two are such devout believers
because I would give anything... anything...
to see you try and explain
your baby-murdering
blood-stained hands
to saint peter.

Out of Date

I want to be out of date
I don't want my children to be able to relate to these words,
born of frustration and hate,
this World full of fanatics
from Whitehouse lawn to Moslem State,

I simply want to be out of date.

The world, its resources and its children
are daily being raped,
half the world still eats from an empty plate.
We idolise consumer goods and drive-by hoods and laws
which strengthen the State.
I simply want to be out of date.

If God came down here he'd say
"FOR FUCK'S SAKE!
I've given you ten thousand years Mankind...
and you've not got past skin colour yet!"

And maybe,
just maybe...

He'd wipe the fucking slate.

I Loved You Like a Brother Till I Found Out You Were a Cocksucker

(or - the arrogance of the homophobe)

Gay!
He's Gay?
You must be mad.
I've known him since we were lads.

Never! Never in the world!
He hung around a load of girls.
He *pushes pooh*?
Pushes Pooh!
Look, I'll twat you mate if I fucking have to.
He's *queer as fuck?*
Queer as folk,
you won't smile long with your fucking neck broke.
Now wind it in. You're having a laugh,
that lad's as queer as I'm giraffe.

Here he comes now. Say it to his face.
Did you hear that mate?
Now tell him, you're straight.

What?

What do you mean… you're not…?

My mate's as straight as Black Lace,
I never could tell from his face,

Never could tell from the way that he talked,
Couldn't even tell from the way that he walked.
He's always been a stand-up geezer.
He put me to bed when I was in Ibiza.

He shared my bed when we were kids
I wonder now what he was thinking behind closed lids.

Then at school we shared the showers,
the times he's seen my cock adds up to hours!
Days!!
And he's GAY!!!

I'm sorry mate.
We've got to part.
I'm not having your eyes on me arse.

I fear deep down you fancy me,
The amount of time you've spent in my company...
What do you mean *"Of course NOT!"*

Hold on mate,
            what's wrong with ME?!!'

Beauty is in the Eye and I Need Glasses

I'm no stranger to the top shelf.
I'm six foot four,
I can reach for myself,
And a simple word in Google can spawn
ten thousand images of internet porn.
All men to this can relate
at least all of those who masturbate.
Cos sex is the thing and it's up for sale,
though not with kids.
That lands you in gaol,
Garry (Glitter).*

An advert for skin cream will cleverly construct
the artistic use of the models buttocks.
And Martini or Bacardi, or whatever the beverage
gives handy pointers on exposing cleavage.
Yet in this age of equality, a man's bare cock, you'll never see
and sad but true,
the neatly trimmed quim
is always kept well within
the panties or nipples behind the wonder bra.
However, a little imagination can carry me quite far
because sex is the thing and it's up for sale
beauty is in the eye and imperfections are being derailed.

There are fourteen year-old girls upset with their tits,
forty year-old women upset with their hips,
small-mouthed women upset with their lips,
and surgeons too ready to snip! snip! snip!
Because sex is the thing and it's up for sale,
from any direction
paranoia will never fail –
just ask anyone in sales.

The young wannabe model is easily posed
after the Doctor re-defines her nose
taking from his bag a meaty chisel
that cuts out all of her natural gristle.

And from the men –
are you good enough for me?
You're not the sort of bird that'd make page three
though you're pleasant, and kind, and with nice to be,
I just prefer juicier tits, you see.

Men – it comes to this!
We shallowly swim in a shallow abyss,
the women we fancy are characterless, all carefully developed
in Quark Express to hide their flaws, and natural contusions,
to create a perfect image, a perfect illusion,
to lead us down the garden path
where the grass maybe green and the dew crisp,
but we don't realise the other side of the fence
doesn't even exist.
Flaws are hidden and images bombard us,
the camera not only lies, it actually retards us.

What about our kids, and their kids,
will they fondly kiss Granny's collagen lips
and wrinkle free botox neck,
will we ever come to regret
dressing our children up in Spice Girls mini's
seeing them copy Britney's schoolgirl shimmy,

and, *"Mum, isn't Rhianna's new top just divine.
I wish I could have her life instead of mine."*
This is where it starts.
The media never mediate.
They crumble your confidence
and just break hearts.

Men, it comes to this,
There is more to life than tits,
Jordan, my love,
You acted too soon,
I loved your little knockers
before they ballooned.
In conclusion I have to say this,
and this, more than anything,
tell and teach your kids –

to be flawed is to be human,
and to be human
is bliss.

** Later changed to Stuart (Hall). Recently over cocaine and coffee a
mate pointed out that it'd transpire ironically that the only people not
fucking kids in the 70's would turn out to be the Gay Rights crusaders.*

MONKEY POET PRESENTS

WELCOME...

ACT 1 ★ TO AFGHANISTAN!

"It's 1839—Watch History Repeat Itself!"

"Deadly historical accuracy and wicked barrages of humour... taken beyond Edinburgh as this show should and must do"
—The Stage

A Stage "Must-See" Show, Edinburgh 2010

Co-Written with John Banks
Directed by Julia Nelson

ACT 2 ★ TO THE UK!

Best Poet, San Francisco
Fringe, 2007+2008

★★★★Eye Weekly Toronto
★★★★CityLife Manchester
★★★★ Three Weeks
★★★★ NUVO Magazine, IN

"near-knuckle"
"breakneck pace"
"funny, raw, relevant"
"no to be missed"
"bullshit-free!"
"hilarious!"

WARNING! CONTAINS WORDS!

PART TWO
The Big Brown Number Two
or
Welcome to the UK (2008)

Welcome to the UK

Welcome to the UK,
where freedom was born
and freedom will stay,
at the top of the agenda.

We don't see the bars on the cage,
because we believe we are free
within the UK.

From the checkout girl who is the wage slave
to the old warrior,
who fought so brave,
yet finds his pension won't pay
his heating bill.

Welcome to the UK,
where celebrity gossip rules the airwaves,
where CO_2 emissions will be shaved
by eighty percent by twenty-fifty,
promised by the Government,
who won't be in power then.
So it's tomorrow's problem – hooray!
We don't have to do anything today!

Welcome to the UK,
where the streets have the sheen and the stink of piss.
Where everyone thinks everyone else lives in bliss.
Where the one thing you don't want but will get,
is a Glasgow kiss.

Welcome to the UK,
from the single mum who sits on the dole,
jabbing heroine into her arsehole,
to the rock star addict on the TV show,
with a thousand groupies waiting to blow him.

Welcome to the UK,
where the crowds and queues in this human zoo,
mean that people don't have that much to do
with each other.
Sixty-one million people,
crammed on this tiny island at sea,
means polite society
is now being mugged,
but not being shot.

Welcome, enjoy your stay,
in the UK.

The Culture

You can tell them by their names,
the Philosopher's Arms,
the Jolly Misanthrope,
the Rabid Dog,
the Brickies' Balls,
the Monkey's Bum
and the Educated Yob.

The Establishments of the town
where old men go to tell tall tales,
talk old toot and drink Newcastle Brown.
The are five fine hand drawn ales,
each with its own frothy golden tale to tell.

The Pub is the hub,
the centre of the wheel,
the grub is pretty good,
but best of all is the spiel,
the chat, the gossip, the view.

There's the Gin soaked optimist –
"It'll end in tears."
The whisky priest –
"If you buy me one, I'll forgive you."
The vodka malcontent –
"Grrrrrrrrrrrrrr."
And the beery economist –
"I'll have two pints of your cheapest, please."

These old men talk and tell
and gape and strut,
giving life to the old line,
*"The people who should run the world
go home when the pub shuts."*

How I Lost my Job

"Tardy," they said to me as I turned up late again,
"It's beyond a joke, beyond a laugh."
I heard him say
as I went down to the Caff.

"What's your excuse this time, Oh Unpunctual One?
Why do I ask?" He said half to himself,
"Let me guess. Your hair was a mess?
The Bus was on fire?
An old lady Hindu had her funeral pyre
in the middle of Rusholme?"

I said, *"Oi, Mouth. Mind the jokes or I'll go straight back home,*
straight back to bed, and I won't come here again to earn my bread."

He said, *"Okay."*

I said, *"What?"*

He said, *"Here are your cards, mate.*
You've had your lot."

It's a buyers market, kids

The House at the End of the Street

Dedicated to the memory of Geoff Platt, a pensioner whose body was found in his flat a year after his death.

Tick, tick, tick, tick,
the sound I always greet
enclosed in this house
at the end of the street.

The sounds of the birds,
caw-caws, shrills and cheeps
are drowned by the traffic
that pours down the street.

People wander past,
and their lives I wish I shared.
People wander past
but my communion stops there
at the window,
the hole into this cell,
this place I cannot leave.
This home become hell.

Tick, tick, tick, tick,
the sound I always greet
enclosed in this house
at the end of the street.
No neighbour comes a-knocking
'cept the kids down the street
who knock my door and run away
on fleet feet

The stairs I cannot manage now,
I'm old and I'm beat,
And I'm just like my house
at the end of my street.

The sun beats down,
the trees wilt away,
My heart and my body
beat on to slow decay
The company I keep
will drive me mad one day

Tick, tick, tick, tick,
The sound I always greet
enclosed in this prison
at the end of your street

Flesh Bang Wallop - What a Picture!

Welcome to historic Fleet Street, the heart of the free press.
The place where the journalists first met
to discuss the stories of the day
but now peddle a different kind of meat.
Read all about it?
Not no more.
Now it's celebrity exposes by the score.

Britney exposes her labial flaps
as she indiscreetly disembarks from a taxi cab.
Kate Moss's moss is on page three
(personally, I don't think that's a waste of trees).
Princess Eugenie nearly shows her Royal Charms.
(In the making of this poem not a single Royal was harmed).

Welcome to historic Fleet Street, the heart of the free press.
The place where the journalists first met
to discuss the stories of the day
but now simply masturbate,
over the paparazzi's latest shoot,
over the paparazzi's latest score.

"Thank God Paris Hilton is a spoilt rich whore –
she's always good for a double-page spread."
Say lazy Editors whilst scratching their heads,
"What the Public wants, the Public gets,
it's not my fault it's mainly breasts."

My Celebrity Crush

I want to fuck Kate Moss,
apparently, she's not up for it.
Well, that's her loss.

I'd love to mate with Kate,
fill her with my being,
take her from here to paradise,
she wouldn't believe what she was seeing.
(Apparently I have a really bad cum face).

But I do want to fuck Kate Moss,
now alas it can never be,
not because of Johnny Depp,
but because of Pete Docherty.

"Kate, love, you've blown it."
Is what I'd have to say,
"Yes, you could have had me girl,
but now there's no way!"

There are lessons that you learn in life,
some so important you write them on the fridge,
one of my personal favourites is,
"Never stir a Junky's porridge."

Porn

There isn't a moral to this story, after all I do masturbate,
just some observations I thought I'd might relate.

A conversation with a female friend of mine
turned to how men have begun to act in bed sometimes.
She said, *"The one thing I cannot stand
is when a man spits on his hand
to lube up my sex.
Frankly it makes me reject them."*

I said, *"They don't do that!"*

She said, *"You bet!"*

Then I remembered a story, the source of which I couldn't place
that said young men had started
to cum on their partner's face without asking.
Just a quick withdrawal,
a money shot shoot,
and a shocked young face
covered in baby-glue.

"And," she said, *"there's been an upsurge
in surgery for the vaginal lips,
to make them tidier, like pornstars."*

I said, *"Have they not seen pornstars tits?
They're like two huge boulders with a giant runway in-between.
They're disgusting. I'm not trying to be mean."*

We agreed, unfortunately, that the Barbie look had caught on.
And there was nothing that I could blame,
except what the internet calls Pr0n.

There isn't a moral to this story, after all I do masturbate,
just some observations that I thought I might relate,
but watching these films now leaves me feeling vexed.
I'd love to see a porno showing love,
as well as hardcore sex.

Love is...

Love is the laughing together,
farting in bed,
comfortable silences,
three words that never need to be said.

Love is being naked,
because love is the truth.
Love is divinity.
Love is everlasting youth.

Love is, *"I'd do anything for you,"*
and Love is the proof.

Love Problem #13 The Blow Job

She sucked me in the morning
until the end of night.
She sucked me down an alleyway,
well out of plain sight.
Her tongue flickered around my bumhole,
and wrapped around my eggs.
When it was all over,
she stood on shaky legs.

"We should be together," she said,
"you'd never have to wank!"

She wiped my sperm from her lips,
and introduced herself as Frank*.

* A true story. Names have been changed to aid the rhyme!

Asylum Seekers
(From the front page of the Daily Express)

They're ruining the towns!
Coming in with their colours,
most of 'em are brown.
"They take our jobs!" scream the mobs
stirred-up by Tabloid Town.

Can't you see?
In ten years time Britain will have no history!
They come here for free!
They're choking the schools, they treat us like fools.
We should be committed!
One Point Two MILLION Asylum Seekers
have recently been admitted!
The wedge is thick, not thin,
we're letting in every Tom, Dick and Harry.
That's One Point Two Million Mohammed's, Wong's or Iraqi's.

The paper does its job, it inflames the mob,
yet doesn't find the space to mention,
that One Point Six Million Brits left
to find a hotter place
to spend their pensions.

St George

"Cry God for Harry, England and St George,"
wrote Shakespeare, the bard,
and made him ours.
The ever ready, reliable, St George
who stuck with us
through two World Wars.

St George, Patron Saint of… Syphilis!
And so we spread, like a disease,
and conquered all of the seven seas.
Bringing civilisation with cutting steel,
a hearty huzzah, and a damn good eye for the other fellows'
real
estate.

For God and Harry and St George,
Patron Saint of Beirut!
There the Dragon he did slay,
in a place aptly called St George's Bay.

For God and Harry and St George, Patron Saint of Leprosy!
And like a leper's skin the Empire cracked,
bits fell off,
the system nearly collapsed.
The pus inside began to weep,
and by the way, St George is also
the Patron Saint of Sheep!

For God and Harry and St George,
Patron Saint of The Teutonic Knights!
The Germans!
I must admit, I was a bit surprised,
but we won't dwell on the wars,
or economic zeal,
instead move on to a different field.

Cutting through the mystery,
let's have a look at this man's history,
St George was a Roman soldier,
from Anatolia,
born late third century,
all sources are however, hagiography,
(which means not the verifiable truth).

In 303
he was ordered to take part in a persecution
but confessed himself to be a Christian,
and criticised the Royal decision.
An enraged Diocletian
ordered torture
followed by execution.
So he was lacerated
on a wheel of swords,
and then decapitated
outside Nicomedia's walls.

For God and Harry and St George!
The shout still outs in the world of sports,
where every shaven head is clad
in the white and red striped flag.
And we still cheer at the sight of the crest,
and despite all evidence
(football, wimbledon etc.)
hold that England is the Best!

For God and Harry and St George, Patron Saint of …

Agricultural workers, archers, armourers,
butchers, sheep, shepherds, field workers and farmers,
Ptuj, the Order of the Garter,
riders, saddle-makers and of course Soldiers!

Canada, Cappodocia, Catalonia, Ethiopia, Ferrara in Italy
Genoa, Georgia, Lithuania, Malta, Modica in Sicily,
Slovenia, Amersfoot in the Netherlands,
Corinthians, the Brazilian Football team, and naturally England!

Equestrians, Palestinian Christians, and the dreadful Syph,
Palestine, Aragon, Beirut in the Lebanon and Venice,
Gozo, Moscow, Constantinople,
Skin Disease, Lod, the plague and Portugal,
Cavalry, Chivalry, Haldern in Germany,
Horses, Horsemen, Husbandmen and Leprosy,
The Scouts, Greece, Herpes, Heide and the Teutonic Knights...

Ladies and Gentlemen,
I give you George,
Patron Saint of everything in sight!

Against My Will

Is it just me, or is the British Army barmy?
I don't mean the soldiers overseas,
I mean the ones who administer it daily.
I hate to go on about the war, but this war has gone on and on,
from 'Mission Accomplished' in '03
to another four killed by roadside bomb.

The Army is understaffed, undermanned
and supplies are badly regulated.
If you're a frontline soldier who has to borrow toilet roll from
the Americans –
you're bound to feel a tad deflated.
And every regiment in the 'Stan has to fill its gaps
with part-time Territorials
who have to buy their own backpacks.
And the Army say they can't afford the right kind of jeep,
so the four are now added to the fifty who died
because Command are playing it cheap.

I know I'm having a bit of a whinge
and liberals can go on and on,
but if you send them in against my will,
at least send them the stuff to get the job done.

Your average squaddie is someone
who believed the Crown needed defending;
or failed at school;
or couldn't join in the rat-race;
or was very good with tools;
or comes from a place where jobs are increasingly hard to get,
twenty-five percent of the UK forces
come from old mining towns. Yet,

I hate to go on about this war,
but this war has gone on and on,
from Mission Accomplished in '03
to another four killed by roadside bomb.

Of the four Soldiers referred to, three were TA and one was the first British female soldier to be killed in action. The TA actually have to buy some of their own equipment and get a really shitty compensation deal, putting that into perspective, a full time soldier gets a shitty compensation deal, the TA therefore get a shitty, shitty compensation deal. The case regarding the unworthy jeeps went through parliamentary inquiry and at the time of writing at least 54 deaths could be held attributable to these. The British Army were referred to as "the borrowers" by the other nations serving in Afghanistan.

Tea

Yes. It was worth the brutality,
the Indian suppression,
for this little bag of bliss,
the Englishman's confection.

You see,
back in the early days
the East India Company
responsible for Britain's tea,
had its own army
to guarantee
the regularity
of supply.

Ah! The cup of tea.
Not only does it taste marvellously,
but you see, symbolically,
even though the contents of the cup may change,
don't think it strange,
that whether fabric, or diamonds,
or oil,
or mineral wealth won through business
or spoils...
It'll all come over like a cup of tea,
whether Chinese, African or Iraqi.
You see –
proper tea is theft.

Gordon Brown, the Man We Thought Would Stop Going Down on America

The first thing we knew he would do,
Was stop cluster bombs from being used,
After all, they kill kids,
And it's true he signed the "No Cluster" agenda,
But then added a tiny addendum.

I said, *"Gordon, what's the clause?"*
He said, *"A Cluster bomb has to have more than ten explosive units."*
I said, *"What?"*
"A Cluster bomb has to have more than ten units."
I said, *"But Gordon, that'll still kill kids."*
*"Ah, Matt, I quite like the CBU 97 that our American friends sell us
to send our enemies to heaven."*
I said, *"I don't know what that is, I'm not trying to be dumb."*
He said, *"Relax, under these new rules it's not a cluster bomb."*
I said, *"What does the CBU stand for?"*
He said, *"erm, Cluster Bomb Unit, but they're very handy in war."*
I paused, *"Gordon, that'll still kill kids."*

There you have it,
Gordon Brown,
the man we thought would stop going down on America.

*This poem proves that sometimes it's good to be wrong. Although
the UK tried to add a note to the cluster bomb agreement signed in
Ireland defining Cluster Bombs as having more than 10 bomblets, and
therefore allowing the CBU97 (bought from the US) to be used, and
managed to get it in the draft, it was dropped (no pun intended) from
the final agreement. As a result, I dropped the poem.*

Politicians

For the love of truth, the righteous they upstand.
Understanding the common folk and how to guide the land.
Caught twixt corporation and the common man.
Knights of the modern age, or will be Knighted if all goes to plan.
Interest rates, budget books and the drums of war,
Need newsworthy sound-bites to grab the votes of the poor.
Greed? A passion these people wouldn't stoop too!

Women are allowed in now – equality takes some getting used to.
Another dull announcement, another dull day,
Needs newsworthy sound-bites to keep the truth at bay.
Knights of the modern age, armed in corrupted steel,
Every politician knows how the voter's really feel.
Robbers, rapists and muggers are held in higher regard,
Sod the politicians and sod their voting cards

Art for Fuck's Sake
(After 10CC)

I just don't understand
how an unmade bed,
a sliced sheep, shark or cow,
or pieces of Elephant shit,
can be held up to be Art right now.

It might be cos I'm thick –
but I honestly think it's shit!

When did the explanation
become more important than the Art?
Why's there an explanation in the Hirst place?
Because it's shit!

This was supposed to rhyme,
but if they can't take the time
to paint a piece that's fine,
that pricks my mind
with wonder,

then I'll follow them instead
and like the unmade bed,
I won't put the effort in.

Do you know how hard it is
to find a rhyme that rhymes

with Tracey-Fucking-Emin.

How to be Patriotic Without Sounding Like a White Supremacist

Ever since I was a kid I felt different.
The only child at school with a Circassian name,
at the height of Reagan and Thatcher's Anti-Soviet game,
made me understand the term, reference and frame
for the word Outsider.

And growing up in society, I noticed the have-nots,
the have not-a-lots and the hypocrisy of the people at the top.
My first time as a protestor was trying to stop Margaret Thatcher
taking away free milk from school – we tried, we failed.

MAGGIE THATCHER! MILK SNATCHER!!
MAGGIE THATCHER! MILK SNATCHER!!
Was the playground protestors' lament.
We were seven, it was worthwhile
and didn't matter that I'm lactose intolerant.
Then watching Ethiopia on the news late
a friend and I ran twenty rounds of the housing estate
to raise money.
And protests on and protests more
and protesting the Iraqi war
I wondered what all my protests had been for…
because they effected no change.

Then earlier on this year something happened to me,
rather cheesily in poetry it's called an epiphany.

Whilst walking down a Manchester street buying my groceries
I said hello to the Pakistani owner
and purchased an African yam.
Then walked down Rusholme's Curry Mile,
past a hundred asian restaurants,
and then further, past a Sikh temple, a Hindu temple,
a Mosque and a Church,
and I saw Britain as a nation
that could one day be without curse.

The first homo species arrived here
nine hundred thousand years ago.
And in the years since that time, a thousand other races
felt that the clime was perfect.
And the British, in always adopting foreign customs
have fostered a British evolution.
The Beakers, the Basques who built Stonehenge with technology
from Spain and Portugal,
Homo Heidelbergensis, the Neolithic's,
the Celts who were originally a tribe from Gaul,
the Belgae, the Romans, the Greeks,
the Jutes, the Frisians, the Saxons, the Angles,
the Danes, the Normans, the Vikings, the wrangles for power
that shaped this land, which gave birth to the modern Britain.
The place that I am from.
And each new wave has been infused,
each bringing different technology and tools,
each all adding to the overall dream,
a United Nation of Outsiders.

The laws have changed and come to reflect the needs of the few
balanced direct with the needs of the many.
From the Magna Carta that originally restricted the Monarchy
to you are innocent, until you are proven guilty.

A United Nation of Outsiders who can learn from each other,
lean on each other,
share the burden with each other.
Not become one with each other,
because that is a glib marketing phrase.
But celebrate Viva la Difference.
That's the richness of this place.
And cramped, congested, overcrowded, busy, dizzy,
Britain is my hope for the future Human Race,
and though we are nowhere near this utopia today,
I'm proud to be striving for it.

I'm proud to be part of the UK.

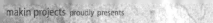

makin projects proudly presents

Developed with John Banks
Directed by Julia Nelson

MONKEY POET IN Welcome to Afghanistan!

It's 1839.
**Britain is going to start a war it cannot win.
History repeats itself.**

STAGE MUST SEE ★

*"A sweeping war epic, plenty of laughs
and a resonant finale."*
THEATRE GUIDE LONDON

*"Comic, brainy and disturbing.
Turns dark tragedy into dark comedy."*
NUVO MAGAZINE, INDIANAPOLIS

*"Deadly historical accuracy and
wicked barrages of humour.
Vividly authentic."*
THE STAGE,
A STAGE MUST-SEE SHOW, EDINBURGH
2010

NEW BOOK
Inapproriate Moral Stories
On Sale Now

August 6-27 (not 16) **13.45** (14.45)

VENUE No. **162**
Sin Club and Lounge
Back Room 207 Cowgate EH1 1JQ
FREE ENTRY   www.monkeypoet.co.uk

makin projects

hoobaadesign

PART THREE
Welcome to Afghanistan.
First performed at The Sin Club as part of the PBH Free Fringe,
Edinburgh 2010
Developed with John Banks. Directed by Julia Nelson.

Adapted from
The Campaign in Afghanistan
A memoir by Lt. John Greenwood
First published in 1844.

I urge everyone to read Greenwood's memoir, he has a
wonderful turn of phrase and his book is an illumination into
the time, covering not only the campaign but his childhood in
Britain and his time in India before the war. The play mirrors
his experiences closely, however being a Lieutenant he wasn't
privy to the actions of the Generals, and their scenes were drawn
from further research.

Lt. Greenwood enters in half-light and stands at ease before addressing the audience.

"When you're wounded and left on Afghanistan's plains
And the women come out to cut up what remains
Just roll on your rifle and blow out your brains
And go greet your Gawd
Like a soldier"

GREENWOOD: *(Salutes)* Kipling wrote that in 1892, years after I was there. Allow me introduce myself, my name is Lieutenant Greenwood. Thank you for attending this evening of recollections from my time in the army and the Afghanistan campaign. If any of you young bucks are thinking of joining up then perhaps tonight will be instructive as to what you may expect.

    Great individuals are often ushered into the world by strange events. Floods, earthquakes, eclipses, that kind of thing. Unfortunately none of these portentous signs occurred at my own nativity. I entered upon this busy universe of ours in a very common-place manner, and after having served Her majesty for twenty years and risen precisely one rank have the feeling I will exit it in a similar manner.

    Mother dearest had always intended me for the church; but on being able to read, I read about the adventures of Bonaparte, Wellington, the great Alexander and dreamed about being a professional soldier. In 1839 I realised that dream.

    Upon joining I was sent down to Cheltenham, and there handed over to a sergeant to be initiated in the mysteries of the drill of a recruit. This was a horrid bore.

SERGEANT: *(Screams at audience)* Attention! Not one of you move, not a single one! Do you consider that appropriate dress for the Army, do you!

    Now Mr A, Head up, if you please sir – shoulders square Mr B! Mr B – you will be asking men to fight for regimental pride sir. They are unlikely to do that unless you are proud! Mr C – very good, but wipe that cocksure grin off your face. You might have been a proper little gentleman at home sir, but, here, you are a proper piece of scum. A proper piece of scum!

GREENWOOD: Now, as disgusting, intolerable, and socially awkward as this is for the distinguished gentleman the best thing to do is give your whole attention to it. It's a necessary ordeal as no officer can possibly reprove an awkward man with any effect when he's known to be deficient himself.

After training us ensigns would put on our smartest uniforms and go into Cheltenham to cast our eyes about for the ladies.

Excuse me madam, would you care for a promenade in the park? Madam? Madam? Oh. Madam, might I buy you a drink? Oh. Madam, I...oh.

Cheltenham has been a garrison town since the days of the Romans and the ladies, having been born and bred there, were rather less impressed with our uniforms than we were ourselves. So we would return, empty handed so to speak, but still full of spunk, we would chat late into the night about the Empire and the only place left where careers, fortunes and glory were to be made... India.

The Governor General of India's residence. The Indian sun swelters outside, a pandwallah fans the room, Parker, Aukland's Aide stands by the drinks cabinet eyeing the gin. AUCKLAND enters.

AUCKLAND: Good God, it's hot. Pandwallah, beat the fan a little faster please, or I will beat you... Thank you. Lord, it's unrelenting...

Parker, the sun is over the yard arm I think. Gin and Tonic. Now, take this down. From Lord Auckland, Governor General of India, to Sir Arthur Wellesly, the Duke of Wellington, Commander of Her Majesty's forces and former General of the Sepoy, that is to say the Native regiments.

Welly,

India is under threat. I need not tell you that her resources, tea, pepper, curry & the Karma Sutra make her the Empire's jewel. Not to mention her actual jewels. However, word has reached me from my envoy in Afghanistan, Sir Alexander Burnes, that a Russian has recently arrived there in court. Not only that but he has been welcomed with open arms by Dost Mohammed, the current Wazir in Kabul.

The Russian Empire is growing and growing hungry Welly. I mean, what's in Afghanistan but sand and shit? Afghanistan's only use would be as a springboard to push here, into India herself.

I have told Burnes to demand that Dost Mohammed expel the Russian immediately and that furthermore he must cease communication with foreign governments unless he acquires our express permission. This Dost Mohammed usurped the throne. The rightful heir is Shah Soojah, who is currently in exile and resides here with me. Let it be noted, the Shah can be reinstated at anytime. I've also asked Burnes to drop that into the conversation. I hope Dost Mohammed takes the point. India, under my watch, will not be allowed to fall.

Seal it, stamp it, send it to Welly!

MESSENGER: Yes sir!

GREENWOOD: *(Addresses the audience)* After training was completed I went to see my CO.

Sir, can I take all my leave now, so I can join the lads in India?

This is actually a formality and the army gives the officer ninety-five pounds to book passage on an outward bound vessel. After packing and suitably attired I went down to the docks.

The Docks: GREENWOOD wanders about, not quite sure what he's looking for, a sea-captain spots him as an easy mark and approaches.

SEA CAPTAIN: Ah-Hah Jim Lad!

GREENWOOD: Who?

SEA CAPTAIN: No matter, young sir. Let me introduce you to the Ariadne, 800 tons Sir, she'll get us there in three months.

GREENWOOD: Where exactly?

SEA CAPTAIN: You have the smell of a man bound for India, sir, a gentlemen of military bearing. The Ariadne will provide you with the finest food, lodging, entertainments, diversions, all for a rate beyond reasonable, I am after all sir, a patriot, It is my English duty to see you boys safe and securely delivered to the East. Tis my misfortune sir that sadly I cannot carry you there for free.

GREENWOOD: How much?

SEA CAPTAIN: 95 pounds.

GREENWOOD:
Coincidence! Well I wasn't born yesterday, we haggled for a while and settled on…

SEA CAPTAIN: 95 pounds. Thank you very much sir. Hoist the Anchor and unfurl the sails!

GREENWOOD: The Ariadne, solid and staunch mistress bore us out to sea taking me on my first steps to my destiny.

What was that? And that!

Many, many times at sea we would see sharks and dolphins play about our bows.

Beautiful, One of the Lord's finer wonders. CAPTAIN sir, Captain, Captain! Can I have a harpoon? *(mimes catching and slicing the dolphin open).*

SEA CAPTAIN: That's called opening the locker, Jim Lad!

GREENWOOD: Who?

Auckland's Residence

AUCKLAND: Bloody weather! It never lets up. Pandwallah! Gin and Tonic, don't drown it Parker. Take this down. From Lord Auckland, Governor General of India to Sir Arth…yes, yada yada yada.

Welly,
        Afghanistan has expelled my Envoy Burnes. Russia and Dost Mohammed get closer and closer. My attempt at sincere and patient diplomacy has patently failed. Action needs to be taken, action now. I have informed Shah Soojah he is to be restored to power. He looked surprised but not unhappy at the prospect. Kept clapping his hands and running round in little circles. I originally intended to raise an army of Afghanistani's to aid him in this task, but that has proved to be surprisingly difficult. Therefore I mean to support him with a force of ten thousand drawn from our own Sepoy and European regiments stationed here. Ex-Envoy Burnes said "We can never win Afghanistan by bayonet alone" but I think that's an unwarrantably gloomy view.

Anyway, he's going back with the Shah. We cannot stand idle. We will not let foreign governments interfere in the running of that country!

Yours in fighting spirit
Brother Auckland.

Seal it, stamp it and send it to Welly.

Messenger – Yes sir!

GREENWOOD: In the three months at sea the captain proved that far beyond the gentlemanly patriot he'd pretended, he was a most niggardly man especially at table, the cheeses dubious, the meats were off and the wine execrable.

But finally, we arrived in Calcutta! As soon as we stepped from the boat we were met with a deluge of people. The sounds of a busy port.

Calcutta Porters.
CALCUTTA PORTER 1: You'll be wanting a manservant sir, SIR! Servant here sir, very good man

CALCUTTA PORTER 2 That man damn criminal sir! Damn criminal man, sir!

GREENWOOD: *(beating them away with his stick)* Gentlemen please, please, give me some room!

One fellow, braver than the rest, kept pointing to pieces of paper he'd sown into his clothing.
CALCUTTA PORTER 3: References sir, character references, good fellow here sir, damn good man.

I read one.

Dear Sir,
        The bearer of this, one Khoda Bux by name is the most infernal scoundrel under the sun; he attached himself to me on my first landing and cheated me in every way he possibly could for a week. On my finding out and dismissing him he had the impudence to ask me for a reference, and I have therefore given

him this in the hoping it may be of service to any gentleman giving the required insight in to his character.

(Beats him away)

Calcutta!

Well, impressive, certainly to me, at the time but... Most Indian cities are very much alike. There is generally a long narrow street with shops on each side which is called the bazaar.

These shops are occupied with dealers in grain, coppersmiths, cloth merchants and manufacturer's of sweetmeats of which the natives are immoderately fond; and the manufacture of which, therefore is a profitable business.

The sweetmeat makers are always dirtier than the rest and to see them prepare their dainty wares is absolutely disgusting. This operation is always performed in public, and it is difficult to imagine how the natives, after witnessing it can make up their minds to eat this mixture of dirt sugar and perspiration.

A bloody great nuisance in these crowded places are these Brahminee bulls. These brutes, which belong to nobody, are actually worshipped by the natives. They generally hang around the grain stores in the bazaar and help themselves to the baskets exposed for sale, and the dealers dare not refuse them the food. So bigoted are the people that they would assuredly murder anyone who injured these creatures, and if a European or Musselman were to accidentally kill one, ha! That would be enough to incite an entire province to open rebellion.

Auckland's Residence

AUCKLAND: Good Morning Parker, my boy. Gin and tonic, have one yourself. What a glorious day. You're up for a commendation, I've had a word with the Generals. Take this down. From Lord AUCKLAND, Governor General of India to … you guessed.

Dearest Welly!

All has been successful. Dost Mohammed has been deposed and resides with me here, ironically in the same suite that Shah Soojah had recently occupied. As for the Shah, he's in Bala Hissar, the fortress at Kabul. Burnes is there too, to…ah, guide him. There are certain things you need to know. Firstly we have ten thousand men now committed in Afghanistan. Mainly in Jellallabad, and Kabul. Our men there are camped outside the city so as not to give the impression of an occupying force.

That's a new tactic Welly, make a note. My turn in the history books I think. The Auckland field deception. The Auckland preventative strike. The Auckland.

Secondly, there have been some calls, especially from the hill tribes for us now to withdraw seeing as we've achieved our objective. Frankly, I don't think Shah Soojah can remain in power without us so the original objective has changed. For the moment we must stay, naturally I can't foresee when exactly we can withdraw. Some of these tribes attacked our convoys in the passes, whilst they ferrying goods from Jellabad to Kabul.

To combat this I have introduced a "subsidy" payment to the chiefs of these tribes. Put that in quotation marks please *(Gestures)* Subsidy. Payments. And while I can't say they've laid down their arms I can say that for the moment - the attacks have now ceased.

Yours rather smugly
Lord Auckland

Seal it, stamp it, send it to Welly.

Messenger – Yes sir!

Mime with messenger taking letter to Welly

The Duke of Wellington's residence.

WELLINGTON: *(Reads letter, holds hand to head)* Watkins, brandy please. Take this down.

Lord Auckland,
As I have said before and will continue to say until a miracle occurs and those who are deaf to common sense, reason and logic will finally listen. "Getting into Afghanistan is easy. Getting out is another matter."

GREENWOOD: Calcutta was still some five hundred miles away from my regiment so I travelled overland to meet them.

India, well? What can one say about the countryside, marvellous, awe-inspiring, aside from the villages of course which are full of flies, fever and filth. We travelled in palenkeens. A team of four runners would take hold of the cot and they'd run along for fifteen, twenty miles. There were relay points at which we'd rest and the teams would swap over, the first lot of fellows going back to their families. Here we would meet fellow travellers, usually in the employ of Her Majesty and we'd go out hunting or trade gossip, not that I had any myself, but it was an education about the land. It was at a relay station I met a Welsh Quartermaster,

WELSH QUARTERMASTER: Hello Boyo, first time here eh?

GREENWOOD: His visage was disfigured and he walked with a limp. Four symmetrical lines across his face, the flesh bubbled through kept behind a thin layer of skin which had grown over the mess beneath.

WELSH QUARTERMASTER: Oh I could tell you some tales, but from the look of you, I can guess which one you want to hear first. Pretty isn't it?

GREENWOOD: Sorry. I meant no disrespect, sir.

WELSH QUARTERMASTER: I know boyo. At ease, I'm quite used to it. Tiger, see? I was out hunting – tiger hunt – see? With my pals. I was fresh, like you. Well, we got into our powdahs, you know, wooden boxes on the back of the elephants. We went out with a few natives as beaters. Going slow and steady in the jungle, when we saw her. Not twenty feet away. For all the orange and fur she was practically invisible in the grass. We shot, and would you believe we all missed! I grabbed my second rifle and as I leant on the wooden to steady my aim, the damn thing swung open and out I tumbled past the elephant and into the grass. Before I could get my bearings it all went dark. And damp. I felt wet breath. My head was in the tiger's mouth see?! Ha! She clawed my leg to lame me – and then I felt her bounce, she'd started towards the jungle depths to finish me for her supper.
     Well, none of my mates could fire, in case they hit me, so I grabbed my pistol and shot her.

GREENWOOD: You killed it?

WELSH QUARTERMASTER: No. She just clamped a little tighter and ran a little faster! At this time I was really bouncing. I grabbed my other pistol and felt around her chest with my other hand, to where I could feel that mighty heart pounding most. That's where I shot her.

Then she dropped dead. And more importantly dropped me. But, she made sure I'd never forget her. You carry two guns? Good lad.

No let me. It's a wonderful place this boyo. Marvellous. Though beware the Hindustani's. More avaricious than the Jews the Hindustani's. They'll steal your bedsheets whilst you're sleeping in them. I mean it, boyo. They sneak up see? They have a feather to tickle your nose with, then as you roll peel out the sheet, just an inch so as not to wake you. Five minutes – another tickle, another inch. Ooh, patient buggers the Hindustani's. Ah, but you'll love this country, boyo!

Plenty of stories and tales to trade on the road. Some true, some not. No let me, you're new. Here's one to get you started. Not one hundred miles away lives a princess. Not Sikh or Hindoo or any type of native, not musselman either. European they say. Married the prince of the region and he died, some say naturally, some not, but that isn't this story. It was said her serving girl, eleven years old, displeased her. I don't know how but I'm sure it wasn't hard to do. The Princess pronounced judgment on the girl, her punishment was to be buried alive.

After the deed was done, the princess knew that as soon as her back was turned, the other servants would dig the girl out see? So she ordered them to bring down her bed from the room, and place it over the very spot where the girl was buried. Then she got into bed and went to sleep, knowing none of the servants would dare disturb her. You can live like a king here boyo, but it's a brutal place, aye, and a bizarre one. Go safe, lad.

GREENWOOD: And he was right. Brutal I would find later, but bizarre. That happened daily.

I continued on my way, looking at this country as a curious mixture of splendour and squalor. Dinapore for example, terrible stinkhole but fantastic for Snipe hunting, a day's march will bring thirty to forty brace. Bowar, Ghazneepore, Muttanapah are excellent for tigers and the deer there are innumerable. The officer can eat very well indeed. I also shot a couple of bears, the pelt of one graces dearest mother's sitting room.

And, whilst hunting one of the bears, I saw this monkey against some rocks, there was something about him. He was almost upright. I took aim, fired. Missed. This time. Missed.

Just getting the bugger fixed between the eyes when my bearers ran up to me screaming "No master, No!"

Turns out it was one of their holy men. You would have expected any human being to move at the sound of the first shots, but not these Holy Men, they're remarkable.

I saw a man near Chazeepore standing in this position (yoga tree) underneath a peepal tree. The natives informed me he had not moved for fourteen years. Upon closer inspection his limbs were quite protracted and if he had tried to use them would have been of no more use to him than if they were made of wood. The nails of his hand, held thus, had actually grown through the backs and protruded some three or four inches out of the back, more like the talons of a wild beast than anything on a human being. He ignored everybody, despite the multitude of people who turned out daily to look at him. He asked for nothing, though I assume he was fed by the villagers who no doubt esteemed themselves very highly indeed that so holy a man had taken up residence near them. Quite, quite mad, the natives!

Auckland's Residence

AUCKLAND: Just the Gin, Parker. Thank you. From Lord Auckland, Gov... From Lord Aukland. To Sir Arthur. Thank you Parker.

Welly,
I have heard of the Tory victory. And received instructions from the new Parliament. It seems Afghanistan is an expense they consider not worth paying for. They have asked for eight thousand of the troops to be withdrawn leaving a skeletal force of two thousand and cut the subsidy's to the chiefs. I fear for our boys. I fear for our Empire. I fear for my entry in the history books. I have resigned my post.

Yours... rather dejectedly
Auckland

Seal it, stamp it, send it to Welly.

GREENWOOD: I met up with the regiment and settled into military life. I got married – oh! And I also received my first promotion. The previous Lieutenant had died of dysentery. It was when I was in India I found out that disease was often more effective for the career than dashing deeds of daring do.

It was also about this time we started hearing things about Afghanistan, rumours that things weren't progressing there as well as we'd ha' liked. At the end of 1841 accounts were received that the inhabitants had risen en masse and beaten our troops on more than one occasion. Bear in mind that the natives had never even heard of a British defeat – we were known to go out onto the field of battle, take on an army ten times our number and win the day with minimal losses. Their name for us was the "Invincibles".

Suddenly we got the order in January 1842 to proceed to Meerut, hailed by everyone as a prelude to a march on Kabul. We had gotten news of the complete destruction of General Elphinstone's army, with it the British Regiment – the 44th. This sent a shockwave through the Empire. Elphinstone wasn't just any old general. He was a hero of the Army. He'd fought with Wellington at Waterloo. We heard the appeal by the widows of the 44th to the regiments ordered on the march, they took a full page advertisement out, I think it was in the Times. They called on everyone to revenge their slaughtered husbands and every heart, native or European responded to that call.

On the march I met Doctor Brydon. He was the only survivor of Elphinstones army and I got him to tell me his tale.

BRYDON: So, you want to hear about it too then, eh?

GREENWOOD: Well yes! If you don't mind that is.

BRYDON: Aye, not at all Sir. It's the curse of the survivor after all, to be a storyteller for evermore. So, do I start at the beginning? When our envoy Burnes was hacked into a hundred pieces, and those pieces paraded around the marketplace like so many other pieces of meat. Do I start there?

GREENWOOD: Well, if you could skip that and go straight to the retreat? If you don't mind.

BRYDON: Of course Sir. Well. There was sixteen and a half thousand of us. Two and a half thousand fighting men. Wives and children of the officers. The rest were just baggage handlers, camp followers, that kind of thing. We set out from Kabul to Jelallabad. Ninety miles.

GREENWOOD: And just you survived.

BRYDON: Aye, Sir. Just me.

GREENWOOD: Did you see many of your mates die?

BRYDON: Aye, Sir I did. I was tending to the sick and wounded after all, for all the good that I did. hose that were lucky died quickly, bullet or blade. Those less lucky, they…just kind of fell by the wayside as the column marched on. Have you ever seen frostbite? Really seen it. It turns the hands and feet into burnt pieces of wood. More than one mate begged me to amputate, but I had no anaesthetic, no antisepsis. We didn't even have tents, for God sake! The temperature in those passes was minus thirty at night. Every morning we would see hundreds of frozen statues. And the column got up, and the column marched, and those that couldn't march were left shrieking in the cold. Occasionally you'd hear a shot as a soldier took care of himself before the Afghans could get to him.

GREENWOOD: Why do the march in the first place?

Brydon: A fine question sir. Why indeed. When the trouble started with Burnes we should have just rode into the marketplace and shot a couple of hundred of buggers, put it down there and then. But we didn't. Elphinstone, dithering, doddery old fool that he was, never gave the order.

Oh' I know all about his reputation, but, Waterloo was thirty years ago. He was eighty-four years old, man. He was senile!

Because we did nothing they got brave, the whole damn city rose up against us.

GREENWOOD: What about Bala Hissar, the fortress, couldn't you…

BRYDON: Yes! We could a ridden up there, raided the city stores and holed up for the spring. We could a done a hundred things. Only one course of action could have doomed us all… and that was the one our glorious leader chose. Idiot.

Those passes were choked with snow, yon high. We had the women and children too. Ackbar Khan, Dost Mohammed's son and heir, he's the man behind all of this. He actually rode out to us, saying "look man, I've got no control over the hill tribes. Give me the women and the children. I can guarantee their safety, I can't guarantee yours."

Well the officers had a meeting and a think the general consensus was "sod off, you savage"

I remember Sergeant James saying he'd rather shoot his wife in the head than pass her over to an Afghan. But that was before the first pass.

It was about a mile long. The Afghans stationed themselves along the crags at the sides. They let us get about halfway down, then they opened up. It was like shooting fish in a barrel.

All order broke down, what officer can think of orders when his wife and children are in the crossfire. No, it was first past the post and the devil take the man behind ye.

By the time we'd got to the other end and counted up… We lost three thousand people in that pass. Ackbar rode out to us the day after, this time the officers threw their families at him. They're still there. Hostages. That's why we're going back.

GREENWOOD: What about the 44th?

BRYDON: That was on the fourth day. I don't know, two hundred, a hundred and fifty men still functioning. The Afghan's had blocked off the front and were gathering at the rear. We all knew that tomorrow would be the last day. That night those that still could decided to make a break for it.

I walked with them and I must've been in a daze because…I suddenly realised I was on my own. The night was still. I've never been so scared. I heard a cough.

"Who goes there?"

It was an old subador, native sergeant. He was holding in his guts.

"Sahib," he said, "I am wounded to death. Take my horse. God get you to Jellalabad safely."

I never even knew his name.

I grabbed the bridle and was just about to mount her when I heard a volley of shots from the hillside. That was the last stand of the 44th.

I got on the horse and rode. I heard shouts. Spotted.

The bullets were whizzing about me, I thought I was dead in a second. I pulled out my sword, shot from my hand. My horse shot in the flank but carrying on. I rode straight for their line.

An afghan horseman came out to meet me. He waved his sword and I ducked. The sword clattered off my helmet, and then I was through. Twenty miles shy of Jelallabad but I rode and rode.

Finally I saw the Jelallabad gate, the horse dropped down dead beneath me. I can remember Corporal Taylor running out to meet me

"Where's the army, sir? Where's the army?"

I said "I am the army. I am the army."

Thanks for the drink Sir. If it's all right I'll just get back to the lads.

GREENWOOD: Brave man. And all of it true. Aside from the bit about the Afghan swordsman. The sword didn't clatter off his helmet. It sheared through taking half his skull clean off.

I didn't see Brydon for the rest of the trip. He didn't seem to want to have much to do with me.

On the rest of the march to Meerut we experienced much annoyance. I wish I knew who planned these things. None of the five rivers of the Indus were fordable. All of our military equipment, camels, horses, artillery and supplies had to be carried in boats. It was a logistical nightmare. For example, it is no easy matter to induce a camel to enter a boat. The camel I believe is the only animal that cannot swim, it is a fact that the moment the lose their footing in a stream, they turn over and make no effort to prevent themselves being drowned.

They just look at you from beneath the water with an expression so stupid only a camel could wear it. When you finally manage to get them onto the boat, many become so alarmed, that they jump off... and are lost. The hump spins them round and drags them down and all you can see is that face, disappearing into the dark

Finally we got to Jelallabad – Akbar Khan's army was besieging the place as we rode out to meet them and they scattered, retreating to the hills. It was one of the most miserable places I've ever seen.

Their army had eaten up every green thing, there was not the slightest sign of vegetation, like a flight of locusts had been through.

As we rode through the gates the band started playing a song of welcome, "Oh but ye've been a long time a-coming". I took the point of course, these men had had it hard.

But we were gathered, cavalry was Her Majesty's light dragoons, 1st & 10th light cavalry, Tait's irregular horse. Infantry, the 6th, 26th, 33, 36th, 38th, 53rd, 60th and 64th regiments of native infantry. I don't believe the people back home know how big the native army is here. I do not know the exact numbers of force but I suppose there were ten thousand fighting men and fifty thousand camp followers.

And we were there. Everybody wanted this war. Everybody needed this war. We were ready to teach the Afghans a lesson and then the order came through. Stop. We weren't going anywhere.

The Governor General's Residence, exactly as it was in the first scene, the Pandwallah idly fans, Parker eyes the gin.

LORD ELLENBOROUGH: Parker, is it? Marvellous. Lord Ellenborough. From London, yes, yes. Oh. Don't mind if I do. Thank you. *(Drinks)* Good God! Where's the tonic in that. I don't care if that's how he liked it. That's why we're in this mess. The man was a bloody drunkard! Now tonic please. Thank you. Parker, did they get the order. Good. Take this down.

From Lord Ellenborough, Governor General of India, to Generals... sorry, what are there names, I'm terrible with Generals... Nott & Pollock, good man. To Generals Nott & Pollock. Congratulations on relieving the force at Jellalabad. Please return to India at once with the men you have relieved. We do not want to be reading about any more British casualties in the press. Whatever hostages there are, we shall negotiate for their release upon your return.

Fold it carefully, warm the wax, press gently, there. Could you? My thanks. How long before we can expect a reply? Good God, that was quick. They said what. I'm the bloody voice of the British Government. Gentlemen, return at once! Good God! This is insubordination! Get Wellington! He controls the army! Why on earth do we leave war in the hands of the generals, it'd be so much easier left to the politicians!

Duke of Wellington's Residence

WELLINGTON: *(reads note, puts head in hands)* Watkins. Brandy please. Take this down.

My dear lord simpleton,. Don't write that."Sir. It is impossible to impress upon you too strongly the notion of the importance of the restoration of our reputation in the east. The loss of the Kabul garrison was the result of either the grossest treachery or of the most inconceivable imbecility and very likely of a mixture of both, as they often go together." The army are there sir. Use them.

The Governor General's Residence

LORD ELLENBOROUGH: He said what? Oh. Right. Parker, take this down. Sirs, "Rescue the prisoners, give proof of British power consistent with British humanity & after so exhibiting the power you are to obey the positive orders of your government & withdraw from Afghanistan."

GREENWOOD: So after weeks waiting in Jelallabad, with animals and men beginning to die from disease, not enough veg for either... finally, finally, we marched.

(Marching beat rises)

From Jellalabad to Kabul,
We fought in 15 actions,
At Gandamack, on the hill,
We found the 44th,
170 corpses that begged for vengeance
Eyes plucked by carrion birds.

We all vowed to pay the afghan's back
With grim determination
Yes, we all vowed to pay the afghan's back
With grim determination

As we travelled through passes,
Some no wider than to a camel
Dragging canon over Elphinstone's dead

We carved a trench of death,
Of retribution
Yes, We carved a trench of death,
Of retribution,

And finally in battle
On open ground
The army proved its worth to a man
Four thousand Afghani's fell on the first day
At a cost of a hundred and ten.

The afghans were shouting "Allah il Ullah"
Their war cry,
"Allah il Ullah! Allah il Ullah!"
And thousands upon thousands
Fell in the battle,
By cannon shot,
Cavalry charge
Musket ,
And Bayonet,
Bayonet!
Bayonet!!

The British army
Is superiority
In every fight!

…And then I saw a sight.

A young afghani boy,
Not more than six
Had a Khyber knife
Longer than his arm
Next to him a fallen sergeant
A brother in arms,
The boy with difficulty holding the knife
Trying to sever the head
Trying to take home his trophy
This memento of the dead.

I saw a comrade go to him
And with his bayonet
Scoop him up without a sound
And toss him from the cliff edge.

"Sir, these savages must imbibe the poison with their mother's milk."

Greenwood goes back to podium, addresses Audience

So we released the hostages. We won Kabul. We returned with honour. As a first campaign went, it couldn't have gone much better for me, but…

No nation but England would take such a country as Afghanistan as a gift. The whole of its yearly revenue is thirty thousand pounds and our expenses there, in this campaign alone, were more than three million. It was said that we needed to take it, in order to prevent the Russians from taking our territories on that side. But I do not see how we have furthered that objective by converting a people who were inclined to be friendly towards us into bitter enemies. By uniting these disparate tribes into a force that now hates our very guts. If you kill a man's child, no matter what the justification, you have an enemy for life. And old Dost Mohammed, the Emir that we replaced. He was released and re-instated. Those on high reckoned he was the only man that could control the place.

It would be laughable but, I remember dragging the canon through those passes, through the soup of human flesh that gathered at the base. Hearing cries in the ranks as someone recognised the face they were stepping into. Every step cracking the bones of good men that had died needlessly.

The history books began to call the campaign Auckland's Folly, which it is still called today. And I'm glad. Because the only consolation I have is that being known as Auckland's Folly, this will never, never, never happen again.

Greenwood salutes.
End.

MONKEY POET'S
MURDER MYSTERY

PBH's FREE FRINGE 2012

A stranger in a strange town... there's amphetamines, a brothel, a bin, oh, and also mass murder...

Guest Starring
Homer, Oscar Wilde,
Charles Bukowski,
Dorothy Parker,
Allen Ginsberg
Special Guest Star
Gil Scott Heron

THE BANSHEE LABYRINTH, VENUE 156, NIDDRY ST
Downstairs, The Chamber Room, 4th – 25th Aug (Exc. 14th)
12.50 Each Afternoon. FREE ENTRY

PART FOUR
Monkey Poet's Murder Mystery

First performed in the Banshee Labyrinth Chamber Room as part of the PBH Free Fringe in Edinburgh, 2012. Directed by Andy McQuade. Developed and toured with public funds via Arts Council England.

Opening Music. The Streets of San Francisco. Patrick Williams.

Monkey Poet walks on-stage into spotlight and impersonates each character as the voice over announces them.

V/O: Murder Mystery starring Monkey Poet. A Makin Projects Production. This week's guest stars: Homer (*frail old man*), Oscar Wilde (*Lasciviously points out a man in the audience for after the show*), Dorothy Parker *(Looks innocent with a Lolita like finger in her mouth)*, Charles Bukowski (*Drunken giving the audience "V" signs*) and this week's special guest star, Allen Ginsberg (*Does half a line of something before he spots the audience, quickly finishes it*). This week's episode, "Good Blood. Bad Poetry."

Lights go up to general wash. The stage is bare except for a chair, no arms, down stage right.

MONKEY POET: *(Downstage, stares with joyful tears out at a remarkable vista)* San Francisco. *(Pause, to audience)* Well, it was in 2007. The last stop on my first fringe tour. I'd come here from Indianapolis. If you don't know, Indianapolis is in the Mid-West of America. I thought it was on the coast. That's cos I had a very small map and Indianapolis is a big word, so the "Polis" bit of the word was dangling in the ocean. I found out it was in the Mid-West the week before I got there. Some performers in Calgary said, "Monkey, you do know Indy's is the Mid-West?"
"Is it? Oh, So?"
"Well, the Mid West is very Republican you know."
"Yeah, so."
"Well, you do that poem about George Bush. The one called 'Fucking Retard'. How do you think that's going to go down?"
"Oh God. They're gonna shoot me!"
But they didn't. The IndyFringe is a lovely fringe, the people are brilliant, it's a very middle class kind of Fringe, it's in a lovely part of the city, and if you're a performer you get treated like a rock star. People are shouting your name from across the street, buying you drinks. I was selling out every single night. I was also giving out two refunds every single night to the morally outraged. I think I'm the only performer in history whose had to give out refunds from a fringe show. But I didn't mind. As I said, I was filling the houses, and I'd actually finally ticked that offensive box I'd been after for so long. Bill Hicks *(crosses himself)* would've been proud.

And that led me here. San Francisco. The Mecca of the Spoken Word. Ferlinghetti's infamous book store, City Lights. Next to it, the Vesuvio Bar where Ferlinghetti, Ginsberg and Kerouac used to get marmalised before taking these amazing road trips down Big Sur, the Pacific Coast Highway. The Purple Onion Comedy Club where Lenny Bruce had played his legendary offensive gigs in the sixties. The Purple Onion, so named, because that was how Charles Bukowski described his own cock. The Purple Onion!

So it was only natural, that with all this heritage and rich history, the San Francisco Fringe Festival should take place in Crack Alley. I'd received an email from them saying "Your technical rehearsal is at 2PM. Do not arrive any earlier. You will not be let in." I thought, that's unusual. And I've been brought up proper, so a little early I found the street that the Theatre was on. And the Street was paved with Crack Heads. *(Points at them while stepping over them gingerly)* Mexican, African American, American Indian, Mexican... Not a single White person among them. *(Checks watch)* A little early. *(Knocks at door)* Come on...

My knocking disturbed a sleeping crack head. He was an old black guy, about seventy, his hair white frizz, but no whites in his eyes though, pure red with black pupils. He came over to me. *(adopts character and walks to member of the audience)* "You ever met the President of the United States? I met the President. I met President Lyndon Johnson. People said to me, what a nigger like you doing meeting the President of the United States? You know what I said? I said "MIND YOUR OWN BUSINESS MOTHERFUCKER!" *(returns to self, shocked, staggers upstage to the door and falls through)* Jesus Christ! Have you seen it out there, man. Holy Shit!

TECHNICIAN: You're early, man. We told you guys not to be early.

MONKEY POET: Sorry mate, I'm... English. *(to audience)* So, we got on with my tech. Now my tech has to be spot on, it's an integral part of the show. To give you an idea on how complex it is... Lights go up, I walk on-stage. I walk off-stage, lights go down. So we got through it in record time. Five minutes later I was seeing the tourist sights of San Francisco. I saw the Golden Gate Bridge... Why's it red? I saw the prison Alcatraz... Oh, it's on an island, I see, yes, that would make it very difficult to escape from! I saw Pier 39... Well, that's just like Blackpool, but with much fresher paint. And then, that time that sets fire to every artists nerve endings. The magical time known as Show-time. *(walks off-stage, announcer voice)* Ladies and gentleman, please welcome to the stage making his San Francisco début, Monkey Poet.

(Sheepishly he enters, nodding and smiling at the audience).

Crikey, not that many here is there? I mean for the Mecca of the spoken word. Doesn't matter. Give us a cheer if you like Poetry? Well, I love it. This one is my banker. It relaxes you all, gets you onside. Let's you know that poetry isn't staid and boring, it can be fun and enjoyable. I bring us all together under the umbrella of love with this one. This one, my first poem, is about me shooting an eight month old baby. *(Breaks out of performance and addresses audience).* It was going OK. The audience were warming up to me, and my nerves were settling down, you know, San Francisco début and everything. And then from the audience.

MAN IN AUDIENCE: This is shit! You are shit!

MONKEY POET: And up he gets and starts to leave. Now with what happened in Indianapolis I shout out after him, "Remember mate, this is poetry. NO FUCKING REFUNDS!" And out he goes. I'm about to carry on when the door opens, and in he comes, but this time he's got a bin full of empty beer bottles and he... *(mimes throw)*. It's a mammoth throw. It clears the audience which is great because the American's are very litigious and I'm there under a false visa. I'm on stage and all I can see is this shape coming out of the light. *(in slow motion he runs to the side)* JEEEESUUS CHRRRRRIST! The venue staff eject him immediately. And I... *(Exits stage in shock)*.

AUDIENCE MEMBER: We want to see the rest of the show!

MONKEY POET: *(Enters slowly, nervously looking between the door the man exited and the audience).* I'm not sure you do... I've not even got to the bit I find offensive. *(Addresses audience)* But I carried on. And at the end the audience gave me my first standing ovation. My only standing ovation. *(Addresses audience member crack head shouted at)*. I'm just saying, if you feel the need, if you think it's good enough, you know, don't hold back on me. If any of you don't believe me by the way, please google "Monkey Poet", "San Francisco", "Trash can psycho" and you can read all about it. After the show I was in my dressing room, relaxing *(sits on chair, in shock)*. And my Tech came in and said the best thing to say in that situation.

TECHNICIAN: Monkey, we are going to get you wasted!

MONKEY POET: *(Standing)* And they did, and I love them for it. Now after the booze and the goodbyes I thought, I need more than alcohol tonight. I need the comforting touch of a lady. And I'd not met any ladies in San Francisco. I'd met a couple of blokes. A lot of blokes. But no ladies. And I thought, "There might be some Ladies in that building there." It was a big pink building. It had the words "Paris Massage Parlour" written in big welcoming letters, and a picture of a lady in a French maid's outfit.

(Enters parlour)

Hi, erm, I'm looking for a Lady. Good. Three... HUNDRED! Right.

She led me down a corridor. And all the way down it there were pictures of people doing things to other people. She opened a door at the end and said. "Take all of your clothes off and lie on the table. A lady will be into see you shortly."

(Takes off clothes and lies on the chair. Taps fingers expectantly)

And in she came. *(stares up in wonder at this vision of beauty mouthing a swearword in disbelief.)* She poured oil on my back an started to rub. It wasn't a very good massage. It wasn't deep tissue or sports therapy or anything, but I wasn't there for the massage. She rubbed at me for about five minutes then she put a box of tissues by my head and left. *(sits up, stares at tissues, stares at door. Realises he's covered in oil and wipes it off. Waits.)* And I waited, and I waited. Ten minutes now. Longer than the actual massage. And then she came back.

MASSEUSE: Have you finished?

MONKEY POET: What?

MASSEUSE: Have you, you know, finished?

MONKEY POET: Erm, I don't think I've started actually love. What about the... you know, extras? *(addresses audience)* And she left. To be replaced by a man mountain. Err, Sorry mate. I asked for a lady.

BOUNCER: Prostitution is illegal in California, Sir. You gettin' ya clothes on or are we calling the Police?

MONKEY POET: What?! What about all them pictures in the corridor...

BOUNCER: Clothes or Police?

MONKEY POET: Hey, I've not just spent three hundred dollars on a five minute massage. I can get a blow job and full sex in Manchester for forty quid.

BOUNCER: You ain't in Manchester any more, Dorothy!

MONKEY POET: Now just you... Hey! Argh! Get off me!

(The bouncer manhandles him and throws him out. He lies crumpled and naked centre stage.)

MONKEY POET: And a metal door slammed behind me.

(Slowly he stands)

MONKEY POET: *(To a passer by)* Evening. You what? Sorry. You want to suck what? No, no, no thanks, mate. I need a drink. Now, opposite the Paris Massage Parlour is the Odyssey Bar. The smoking ban has been in effect in California for four years, but there is smoke pouring out of these windows and I think, perfect.

(Enters Bar) There's a Chinese waitress behind the bar, playing dice with one of the customers. "Excuse me, love, could I have a large Brandy please? Yes, I know, I'm putting them on. *(Dresses)* Cheers. Is it all right if I smoke?" And she passes me a sweetie tin. I look around the bar and all the other customers are using the tins as ashtray's. And then I twig. What happens is, if the police raid the place, you put your ciggie in the sweetie tin, snap it shut, and the police assume your having sweeties with your

brandy, presumingly ignoring all this *(wafts smoke away from his face.)*

I sit down and take stock of my San Francisco experience so far. What did I say, I mean actually say, to make a man throw a bin full of glass at me? Why in San Francisco is it so hard to get a blow job... from a lady? I'm thinking this when a woman runs in off the street, grabs my brandy from the table and runs out, I go, "Oh, come on!"

The Chinese Waitress throws her dice holder at the closing door shouting "F'tin too wah!", which I assume means, please bring back the glass when you have finished.

(Pause. This is a significant pause because we are now leaving reality. Monkey Poet has entered the rabbit hole so to speak, the magical poetry place of the Odyssey Bar, being the doorway to this realm.)

DYLAN THOMAS: Oh, she got you there, didn't she, eh, Boyo?

MONKEY POET: Yeah, it looks like she did.

DYLAN THOMAS: English, is it? What brings you this side of the water?

MONKEY POET: Poetry, mate.

DYLAN THOMAS: Poetry? Bloody hell, me too, and the lads. I'll get this one. Susan, Susan, can I have another Brandy here please.

MONKEY POET: Look, mate. I'm not being funny, but who was she?

DYLAN THOMAS: Oh, she's one of the homeless. They're mad, man, nuts. What happened, you see, Reagan, back in the eighties, to save some taxes, shut down all the public institutions and they just turfed all of the patients out onto the streets. It's rather sad really.

MONKEY POET: Bloody Hell.

BUKOWSKI: Hey, Dylan, man. We gotta go. We are running late buddy, we are running late.

DYLAN THOMAS: OK Charlie, got a plus one here. Poet don't you know. What's your name, Boyo? Monkey Poet? Well, it takes all sorts. This is Charlie Bukowski, over there we've got Percy Shelley, Rabbie Burns, Bill Shakespeare and I'm Dylan Thomas at your service, Sir.

MONKEY POET: You what?

DYLAN THOMAS: Hurry up with that drink, Boyo. Taxi!

Monkey Poet sits on the chair, evidently now a seat in a taxi.

BUKOWSKI: So, Dylan tells me you're some kind of poet. What kind of shit do ya pour? Is it honest? Is it truthful?

MONKEY POET: Well, Mr Bukowski. What I like to do, is sort of put society on stage you know. Let the audience see it for what it is, you know, the truth as searchlight...

BUKOWSKI: Jesus Christ, I think I'm gonna puke.

SHAKESPEARE: Is it dramatic? Does it have a sense of urgency?

BURNS: Och, shut it Shakespeare, you wee poof, dramatic, urgency. Tell me laddie, is it dirty? I've written a corker called "Nine Inch Will Please a Lady." And let me tell you son, it bloody well does. I've written another called "Cock Up Your Beaver." But don't get too excited, the meanings of words change over the years, it just means, put a wee smile on yer face, lad, you know.

SHELLEY: Rabbie, must you always think with your penis? Tell me, Sir, will your poetry inspire the masses to rise?

MONKEY POET: Well, Shelley, Percy? OK, Shelley. I do this one right, it's about me, right, it's about me shooting a baby.
SILENCE

SHELLEY: Oh. That sounds... very... erm... post modern. We're here, I think.

They exit taxi.

MONKEY POET: *(To audience)* And it was a big old Agatha Christie style mansion, right up in the hills, by the Ivory Tower if anyone knows San Francisco, looking down over the whole city.

DYLAN THOMAS: Come on! Open up! You can't start the party without us!

SHAKESPEARE: I've written this piece about a man opening the door in the middle of the night. It's very funny, set in the middle of a tragedy, like. If you are doing a tragedy, throw in a couple of comic characters, keep the whole thing ticking along. And if you're doing a comedy, dick and fanny jokes. Audiences love dick and fanny jokes. Have you heard of my play "Much Ado About Nothing"? Yeah, it's an anagram. It's a fanny joke. "Much ado about an 'O' thing. Yeah, 'O' thing, Vagina. Remember, Fanny is Funny.

MONKEY POET: *(To audience)* And the door opened.

GIL SCOTT HERON: *(In a Tom character voice, see undoubtedly stereotypically racist Hollywood films of the 30's for guidance).* Well, hello there, Mass'ers. Come on in, can I take your coats? Say, do you need a hand with Mr Bukowski?

MONKEY POET: Wait a minute, aren't you...?

GIL SCOTT HERON: *(In his own voice)* Gil Scott Heron, yes I am. I'm stuck with this Goddam Tom character until the sixties. That's when I get to finally use my own voice. Until then it's a white man's world. But I tell you. The day'll come when those Mexicans realise just whose been fucking them over all these years, and they'll stop killin' each other and bring their machine guns up north, and all the pained and homeless on the streets of this great nation of ours, will take that pain to the gates of the White House and I tell ya, the revolution will be live, brother, the revolution will be live. But until then...*(Resumes Tom).* Climb on my back Mr. Bukowski. There you go. Follow me, Gentlemen. *(Sings)* Swing Low, Sweet Chariot...

MONKEY POET: *(To audience)* And I was led into a great hall ram, jam, packed full of people. And Dylan started pointing them out to me. Aristotle, Chaucer, Pope, Emily Dickinson, Anne Sexton, Sylvia Plath... with Ted Hughes. Every poet I'd ever heard of and hundreds that I hadn't. I'm more of a doing poet that sitting down and being academic poet. And frankly, after the disappointment of the Paris Massage Parlour I was keeping a close eye on the male-female balance and unfortunately it all looked a little...

OSCAR WILDE: Cock heavy, isn't it? Perfect if you like heavy cocks.

MONKEY POET: Whoa! Who are you?

OSCAR WILDE: Wilde, Oscar. And you?

MONKEY POET: Monkey Poet.

OSCAR WILDE: Delicious.

DYLAN THOMAS: Now, now, Oscar. Keep it in your pants. Think about the Missus.

OSCAR WILDE: In Marriage, three is company and two, none.

DYLAN THOMAS: Very pithy, Oscar. Are you pithy, Monkey? You have to be nowadays, you know. Everything's bloody quotations. If you go on longer than three sentences, people can't remember what the hell it was you were going on about. Let's mingle shall we.

MONKEY POET: Who's that guy on his own, Dylan?

DYLAN THOMAS: Oh, that's Tennyson. No one speaks to him any more. Not since that "Charge of the Light Brigade" nonsense. Did you read it? Patriotic drivel. "Into the Valley of Death" blah, blah, blah, turned a stupid butchery into a romantic tragedy. But he's very pithy though. In all the bloody books, as is Oscar, as is... Ah, Dorothy!

MONKEY POET: *(To audience)* Dorothy Parker was stunning. Her eyes witty and intelligent. Her skin radiant. And she walked in beauty.

DOROTHY PARKER: Well, I never liked a man I didn't meet. Tell me, how's life in the literary world.

MONKEY POET: *(Bashful)* I'm not really part of the literary world.

DOROTHY PARKER: But Poetry's still popular, isn't it?

MONKEY POET: *(Pause. Sees Gill Scott Heron with a drinks tray)* Ah, Gil, drinks. Brilliant. How you getting on, Gil?

GIL SCOTT HERON: Have you had a look around here, Monkey? One Black person and I'm the Goddam Butler. There's no Harlem renaissance, no Jean Toomer, no Claude McKay, no Langston Hughes... You got no idea who I'm talking about do yer?

MONKEY POET: Yes, but that's not racist Gil, I don't know who half these fu... Would you like a drink, Dorothy?

DOROTHY PARKER: I'd like to have a Martini, two at the very most, at three I'm under the table, at four, Monkey... I'm under the host.

MONKEY POET: Have you got any Martini's, Gil?

GIL SCOTT HERON: Nope, just got these Ambrosia's. Well, White-Russian's, closest thing we could get to Ambrosia.

MONKEY POET: Great. Two of them, please. Who's that guy, Dorothy, the dude in the toga?

DOROTHY PARKER: Shh! That's Homer. The Father of Poetry.

HOMER: *(Taps his glass calling for silence)* Has everybody got their drinks? Good, good. Then I'll begin. Poets, Bards, Storytellers. It is my honour and privilege to welcome you here tonight. The Word has risen with the World, gaining in complexity to better reflect the complexities that surround us all. The Poet, or any artist for that matter, is the Weathervane atop Humanity's house, it is his function to indicate which way the wind is blowing. A valuable occupation indeed, as long as Humanity continues to listen. Poets all, I salute you.

Homer toasts the assembled guests and they drink. Aside from Monkey Poet who sniffs at his.

MONKEY POET: Dorothy, what's in this?

DOROTHY PARKER Vodka, Kahlua and cream.

MONKEY POET: I can't drink this. I'm lactose intolerant. If I drink milk or cream I vomit immediately, and that's if I'm lucky. If I'm unlucky it goes straight through my system and I shit myself. Dorothy? Dorothy, come back...

OSCAR WILDE: Monkey, you smooth talker, you. Tell me, how was your performance tonight?

MONKEY POET: I got a bin thrown at me.

OSCAR WILDE: Quelle Surprise. Oh, don't take it like that. Sounds like a story, eh? A bit of gossip never hurt anyone. There's only one thing worse in the world than being talked about, and that's etcetera etcetera. Look at me. They put me, Me, in prison for Homosexuality. They closed my plays in the West End, took my name down from the billboards. And with that sentence, Monkey, they tried to kill me. Certainly no man of my class had ever survived a sentence like it. And what was the result, hmm? Two best-sellers in the Ballad of Reading Gaol and De Profundis, and surrounded by as much sex-starved cock as I could manage while writing them.

Look at him. Look at Shelley. He wrote the Masque of Anarchy and Merry Men of England, poems which called for the working classes to rise and break free their shackles. What did the Establishment do, hmm? The moment he died they rewrote History painting him as a rose-sniffing Romantic, a fop. But, then what happened? Ghandi used to recite the Masque of Anarchy to thousands of his followers, on a different continent, in a different century. If you want to be a real Poet Monkey, you best prepare yourself for some stick.

Ah, here comes Byron. He did say he wanted a word. Look, don't mention his foot, he's sensitive. And, Monkey. Later on, if you find your bread isn't buttered on Dorothy's side, just tip me the wink and we can take it upstairs any time you fancy. Toodle-pip.

BYRON: *(Enters limping)* Ah, Monkey. How do you do? Don't look at the foot! A pleasure to meet you, Sir. How's the world of poetry, eh? Good God, Man. Back in my day it was all the fanny you could eat and all the Laudanum you could stomach. If there was a whisper you were in town there'd be calls, parties, affairs, soirées. Jesus, the publicity alone. Still like that is it, you lucky bastard?

MONKEY POET: Not really. No.

BYRON: Pity. Heard you had a bit of a fracas with a bin. Does you good to rile up the cretins once in a while. Ever been to House of Lords? Jesus. I remember my first speech there. During the time of the Luddite rebellion. You know, men smashing up the machinery that was putting them out of work, and of course, no work means no money, no money means no food, no food means children, children literally starving on the streets and these idiots in Ermine blind to it all. Being ferried around from one stately home to another stately home and never opening the curtains along the way and I said to these... these... "Gentlemen," I said, "You are breaking the same laws that you are so murderously defending. Oh, maybe not smashing machines, no, but fraud, eh? Illegal bankruptcies, eh? Felonies, eh? If you punish one crime you must punish the other. You all defile this House." You know what they said when I finished speaking? Nothing. Just carried on with the next order of business like I hadn't said a word. Ah, Master Heron. Drink, Monkey? *(takes two drinks from Gil Scott Heron and giving one to Monkey Poet and toasts:)* Man as a reasonable creature must get drunk, the best of life is but intoxication. *(He drains his in a gulp).* Ah, here comes Dorothy. I'll leave you to it, you lucky bugger. *(He exits).*

DOROTHY PARKER: *(Approaching Monkey Poet)* So, what did you make of Byron? Slept with his Sister, you know? And Ginsberg over there will sleep with virtually anybody. And you know Oscar. Two children, happy-ish marriage, but still, an eye for the boys. If you want to be a real Poet, Monkey, you have to be fairly depraved sexually. Are you? Depraved?

MONKEY POET: *(Thinking)* Depraved? Erm. Dorothy. Have you ever seen Two Girls One Cup?

She leaves in disgust, he goes to follow but turns in anger at himself. Closes his eyes.

MONKEY POET: FUCKING HELL! Oh, hello Homer.

HOMER: Hello, sorry, who are you?

MONKEY POET: Monkey Poet.

HOMER: Oh, and what is it you do do?

MONKEY POET: Performance Poetry.

HOMER: Oh, nice. Audiences?

MONKEY POET: *(Looking at audience)* They're OK, yes.

HOMER: Money?

MONKEY POET: Enough to keep the wolf in the porch.

HOMER: No fortune then. How's the fame?

MONKEY POET: I'm not in danger of being publicly mobbed.

HOMER: Yes, there's no money in poetry... but no real poetry in money either. Ha ha ha. Ah, TS Eliot, meet Monkey Poet. Monkey Poet this is...

TS ELIOT: We've met.

MONKEY POET: Have we? I don't recall...

TS ELIOT: Well, I've seen you at any rate. I saw you earlier on this evening. You were performing. Like a little Monkey.

MONKEY POET: Oh, not much of a fan then?

TS ELIOT: *(Barely contains his anger, which rises threatening to break completely throughout this scene)* It was, it was fucking disgusting, man. What the hell was that about shooting a baby? And no rhyming schemes at all, Homer, just da-dum-da-dum-da-dum-da-dum-da-dum. You know nothing about poetry, man, nothing.

MONKEY POET: Hey, easy.

TS ELIOT: What's a Villanelle?

MONKEY POET: Erm.

TS ELIOT: How do you write a sonnet?

MONKEY POET: Erm. That's fourteen lines.

TS ELIOT: What's the rhyming scheme?

MONKEY POET: Erm.

TS ELIOT: Trochaic Pentameter?

MONKEY POET: Sorry, I've not met him.

TS ELIOT: What! OK, we're going to leave form. What about content? Byron, over there, what of his have you actually read?

MONKEY POET: Erm.

TS ELIOT: Dylan Thomas, over there, what of his have you actually read?

MONKEY POET: I've read Under Milk Wood, well, the introduction to it anyway.

TS ELIOT: What? You never even listened to the Richard Burton version. Jesus Christ, and you call yourself a poet!

MONKEY POET: I don't, I don't call myself a poet, I'm more jokes that rhyme.

TS ELIOT: What's your fucking name?

MONKEY POET: Monkey P...

TS ELIOT: HA! I was expecting the world to have changed Homer, but not like this, not with this, I dunno, I just blew, I saw red... I... I... picked up the trash can and I...

MONKEY POET: You threw the bin?

TS ELIOT: You're lucky I didn't break your fucking legs!

MONKEY POET: Yeah! YEAH! Well at least I didn't write fucking Cats!

TS Eliot swings at Monkey Poet who ducks and retreats in fear. Oscar Wilde enters.

OSCAR WILDE: Monkey, Monkey, come quickly. You've got to help me, come on.

They run into the Hallway and up the stairs.

MONKEY POET: Where...?

OSCAR WILDE: Bukowski's trapped himself in the toilet. It was all going beautifully. I was just helping him with his pants when... Oh! Hello Ginsberg, how are you?

Allen Ginsberg is at the top of the stairs. He's sweating and shaking. His hand strokes his arm in the time honoured fashion of the junkie.

ALLEN GINSBERG: Um, yeah, look, do any of you guys want any amphetamine, or, you know, maybe a blow job?

OSCAR WILDE: *(pause)* Erm, Monkey. Would you mind taking care of Bukowski for me? I'm just going to nip into the other room and have a little chat with Uncle Allen.
MONKEY POET: Sure. *(Approaches bathroom)* Bukowski? You in there, mate? Are your pants up? I'm coming in. You sure you're ready?

Monkey Poet enters bathroom. Bukowski's head is in the toilet bowl, his bum in the air.

MONKEY POET: Bukowski... Your heads in the toilet... I'll just take your head out of the toilet.

He does so and is shocked to find Bukowski dead. He recoils from the body and runs back onto the landing. He rushes into the room that Wilde and Ginsberg retired to.

MONKEY POET: Ginsberg, Wilde, something's happened to... Wilde? Ginsberg?

They are dead. He runs back down the stairs and into the ballroom.

MONKEY POET: Dylan, something terrible's going on... Dylan? Chaucer? Tennyson? *(As he speaks people in the room drop dead one by one like dominoes)*. Dorothy? NO!

Everyone in the room is now dead except for Monkey Poet. Homer sits slumped on a chair, his eyes open, yet glazed. Monkey Poet approaches him and waves his eyes over the old man's face. Gradually Homer's eyes focus.

MONKEY POET: Homer? Homer? What's going on? Everyone's dead.

HOMER: Poetry should be for everyone. But it's not. Poets just publish to be read by other poets nowadays. Far better to consign ourselves to the dustbin of History than be endlessly dissected in classrooms by bored students. A decision had to be made, and I as the Father of poetry made it.

MONKEY POET: But that's... that's... I hate to paraphrase Eliot, but I'd much rather go with a bang than a whimper.

HOMER: What do you think this is? It's the best bang I could muster. Oh well, we'll both be dead in about thirty seconds anyway. It's a pity about poetry, dying the slow death of indifference. I should have been a builder. There's something so solid about brick. Nowadays our words just rot in anthologies that no one buys.

MONKEY POET: But Homer... That's wrong. Poetry's a piece of piss. That's the point. Everyone can do it. You don't need to develop characters, you don't need a narrative arc, you don't even need to use proper grammar.

HOMER: Proper Grammar, what? Why are you still alive?

MONKEY POET: I've got no idea.

HOMER: You did drink the ambrosia?

MONKEY POET: No, no, I'm lactose intolerant. If I drink milk or cream then I vomit immediately, and that's if I'm lucky, if I'm unlucky it goes straight through my system and I shit myself.

HOMER: Good Gods... Poetry's stuck with you!

Homer dies. Gill Scott Heron enters and surveys the scene.

GIL SCOTT HERON: Well Monkey, looks like it's just you and me. Homer's dead. And he was dead wrong. A Poet's work is to name the unnameable, to point at frauds, to take sides, start arguments, to shape the world and to stop it from going to sleep. And there are plenty of poets out there doin' that. You know nothing Monkey, I mean, nothing. Abdelmoniem Raham, he's poet from the Sudan, he was arrested in September 2011. Sentenced to death. Not even his solicitors know what the Goddam charges are. Habib Ali Al Matiq, poet from Saudi Arabia, arrested in February last year. Again, no charges. Even the Nobel Peace Prize Winner, Liu Xiaobo, was sentenced to eleven years in 2008 for criticising the Government. The Nobel Peace Prize Winner, man. They could all be being tortured as I speak to you now. And before you say, well that's over there, over here, in the USA, the former Poet Laureate, Robert Hass, a seventy year old man was beaten by the riot police with truncheons at the Occupy protests at Berkeley, the home of the free speech movement. You've got to use your voice for the people that don't have a voice. No one out there hears silence.

MONKEY POET: How come you're still alive Gil?

GIL SCOTT HERON: You don't think these racists would give me a fuckin' drink, do ya? I'll see you around Monkey.

MONKEY POET: So we said our goodbyes and I walked away from the mansion, down the hill, through the streets of San Francisco and headed for my venue. I got to the street it was on, stepping over the cracks and the crack-heads, the Mexican, the African American, the American Indian, the discarded, the dispossessed, the disenfranchised. And disenfranchised made me think of England, where people had the Vote, but they were never heard because they didn't have the money to buy the word of a politician. I thought of what Gil had said. I remembered reading an interview with a Nigerian poet, he'd been locked up for four years, and he described the tortures that he saw. He described people getting their bollocks nailed to tables.

When I got to the venue there was a crowd outside. One of them pointed and said, "That's who we're seeing, the Trash-Can Guy". And that became my nickname in North America. Oscar was right. A little gossip never hurt anyone. And I was glad to have an audience, because after everything that Gil had said, I really had something I wanted to say to them. I was still going to start though, by shooting a baby.

Blackout

The Monkey Poet

"This audience were in stitches.
THREE WEEK

"Working Class Socialism.
throwback to the 80's an
that's no insult
SCOTSMAN

"The darkest, rudest an
Funniest thing you will see.
BROADWAY BABY

"A tour-de-force
VENUI

"Barrages of humour
THE STAGE

"Many laughs
LONDON THEATRE GUIDE

"Thoroughly Entertaining
DAILY INFO

"Funny, furious and filthy
Dominates the stage.
JERSEY EVENING POST

PBH's
FREE
FRINGE
2013

5.10 PM Daily 3rd-24th Aug (Exc Tues). Venue 156
BANSHEE LABYRINTH, Banqueting Hall, Niddry St. EH1 1LG

PART FIVE
The Monkey Poet

First performed at The Banshee Labyrinth, Banqueting Hall as part of the PBH Free Fringe in 2012.

God Knows

Cos you've got to admit,
God is a little odd,
a bit of a sod if the truth be told.
I mean look at the works He doeth,
behold – famine, disease, death, destruction and decay.
These are not good ideas, not ones to sway me into supporting
Him,
in fact, they lead me to doubting Him, omnipresent,
manifest,
His actions have got him being closer pegged
to being some sort of reject
on X-Factor or Big Brother.
Petty, callous, yet thinks Himself perfect.

See Him now... in the Big Brother Kitchen.

"Adam's eaten that apple.
Adam's eaten that apple.
I told him not to,
I said, take a piss in the sink, if you have to,
but, don't touch that bloody apple.
Do you know what he's done?
Do you know what he's gone and done???"

And God spits His omnipresent dummy
out of His universal pram, and says,
"That's it. Fuck Man!
This is what it's like to get older,
here, have a dose of Ebola.
Let's make children into soldiers,
I've told you Mankind,
it's my way or the highway,
those are the rules and they're OK
by Me!"

Cos you've got to admit,
God's a little odd,
a bit of a sod,
just ask Job.

Hors D'oueveres

At my perfect dinner party,
Richard Dawkins was explaining to God,
why He didn't exist.
God took it on the chin and said,
"No, dear Richard. Without me you wouldn't exist."

Dawkins said, "No, no, no. Without me, you wouldn't exist.
You are a construct. A belief embedded in thought
to help Man cope with the cold emptiness of the Universe."
And God said, "Richard, Richard, the Universe isn't that cold,
the Sun is ninety million miles away and
can tan you very well.
Go to the Sahara, Richard."
And Dawkins replied, "Go to Hell!"
God said, "Been there, seen it, done it."

Dawkins threw his drink over God.
God said "Why you!"and pulled back his smiting arm.
Dawkins said, "Come on then!"
I said, "Hey, hey, this behaviour is unacceptable.
I wish you both didn't exist,
you are both equally troublesome to the appreciative atheist.
Now leave!"

Looking back on it, my dinner-party was not that perfect.

An Open Letter to All Faiths and Religions

Sell the churches, smelt the crosses,
e-bay the clothes and the crooks of office,
flog the jewels and the estates
act now before it's too late.
For the wars that you've caused,
for the hatred and the grief,
for the homophobia and the massacres done for your beliefs.

For all of the hypocrisy, for the torture in your name
for fiddling with children
and never shouldering the blame.
Rid yourself of all your vestments,
kiss goodbye to every single church
and give all the wealth you accrue
to the poor and starving on the earth.

With this gesture acknowledge that it's time now to move on
not least because we've finally found the Higgs-bosun
– probably.

Live now for humanity, consolidate and cancel debt,
concentrate on helping and consigning the regrets
to the dust bin of history,
the folly of youth,
now that we as a species have reached maturity,
prove that you have too.
Take this chance to wipe the slate clean
of paedophilia, intolerance and inquisition
and when you die and meet your makers,
you may even be forgiven.

ESA (or They Don't Give ATOS)

So they send you a form
and you try to fill it out
getting all the evidence together
to give it some clout,

they get that and get you
for your medical check
to see if you can work or
need support below decks,

and they put you in a group so you don't pass go.
don't get your money so your morale's pretty low.

Cos you know you can't work,
you're on a dialysis machine
but they need 20% in cuts
they don't think of your liver or your spleen,

and you can't accept their judgement
so you go to appeal,
then they have to follow protocol
to keep it nice and legal.

So they send you a form
and you try to fill it out
getting all the evidence together
to give it some clout,

and what does it matter if a few fall by the way
that can't live with the pressure of the ESA.
The numbers come down, a new policy is borne,
the sick and disabled are being euthanised by forms.

Turning the First Corner

Nervously tasting the freedom as
I leave my father's guiding hand
at each pedal push the sun slicked street
glides quicker

I can smell the cool breeze
as it whistles past my ears
though they're also responsible for my balance
which completely fails me
as I misjudge
         that
            first
         ever
     corner

the tarmac scrapes hands and knees
tears begin to well inside
but my father's voice,
"well done son,"
stops them from rising
to be replaced
with my first bit of pride.

A little shaken I dust
down my pants
pick up the bike
and walk back tall

the only time in my life
that pride came after a fall.

Mr Twit

Mr Twit tweets twat-loads of shit.
Mr Twit is it! Mr Twit is sick of that 'n' this 'n' this.
Mr Twit thinks thoughts that no-one ought
and spews them forth
in a torrent of bile
mile after mile of 140 character bits.
Mr Twit thinks this.
Mr Twit tweets that.

Mr Twit only knows he exists because
another twit re-tweets Mr Twit's tweets to sheep
or "followers" as they are called
in this existential Rome
the new home for virtual democracy
where every voice is heard
140 character herd of silent cacophony.

Though occasionally big stories don't trend,
Mr Twit's twitter does not want to offend
the stock exchange on which it depends to float
Mr Twit's twitter is the shiny face-bucked new gravy boat.

Mr Twit tweets his torrent of thoughts
unaware that libel laws apply.
Mr Twit didn't study publishing.
He's too busy rubbishing
all the things that to him matter
The Voice, Britain's Got Talent, Footy and Sep Blatter.

Mr Twit tweets on blinkardly throughout the day
the gravy boat floats merrily on its way,
cos Mr Twit & the Tweet Sheep don't democratically matter
the only gravy Mr Twit'll get are the brown splatters..

Signs

We've all seen the signs, and no one pays attention.
Do not cross, respect your boss...
millions of signs
too many to give all a mention.

We've all seen the signs
discussing them becomes irrelevant
I know, we know , we all know
but who pays attention?

We can all see the signs
as oceans acidise
and coral reefs die
as factions tribalise
as the disabled in this country commit suicide
as common decency nose-dives
as corporations politicise
as 150 year old freedoms
are taken before our eyes.

We can all see the signs
– the robbery of the NHS,
they privatised half the beds
by putting the hospitals in such a financial mess
they have to hire them out to stave off the distress of closure.
Reforms by Thatcher
borne by Blair
concluded by Lansley.

We can see the signs
when poets and bands are imprisoned
when comics are killed
we can see the signs,
and sorry to say to those who
want a revolution
as Dylan said,
"the times have changed."

It's the rich who have built
the barricades
in gated communities,
privatised the police,
to protect their profits and their people.
It's a golf club that we can't swing
and we don't belong to,
a 21 trillion moneyed laundered and cleaned club.

We can all see the signs

Else Lasker, a Jewish German,
my favourite ever poet said,
"the true poet does not say azure, the true poet says blue."
Meaning don't say do you mind, say FUCK YOU.

On Hitler's rise to power in '33
she saw a group of Nazis
raise a Jewish garrett
or she was beaten by them with sticks
historians don't know which,

but at age 66
she didn't go home
she jumped a train and didn't look back
headed off down the tracks cos she saw where it was going.

She saw the signs.

We all see the signs.

She did something.

We have to,

fight or flight?

Remember, this is a democracy – that choice is yours.

hurts
LOVE ACTUALLY

Directed by Andy McQuade
(Fringe Report, Best Director 2012)

THE UNOFFICIAL SEQUEL TO THE HIT FILM

FREEEEEEEEEEEEEEEEE SHOOOOOOOOOOOW
3rd - 24th August. 12.50PM Daily (Exc. Tuesday)
The BANSHEE LABYRINTH, VENUE 156
NIDDRY ST, 'Twixt High St & Cowgate

Photos Luke Walwyn   Design Jez Cowley

PART SIX
LOVEhurtsACTUALLY.

First performed at the Banshee Labyrinth Chamber Room, as part of the PBH Free Fringe in Edinburgh 2013. Directed by Andy McQuade. Developed with public funds via Arts Council England.

Opening Music – *Pissing In The Wine*, Chumbawamba

V.O: Love hurts Actually, the unofficial sequel to Love Actually, that's right, unofficial... so you can't sue, Mr Richard Curtis! Or, if you can, please don't, the writer hasn't got a pot to piss in. And here he is. Ladies and Gentleman, Monkey Poet.

Guest Starring:
Emma Thomson as Emma
Alan Rickman as Alan
Liam Neeson as Liam
Martine McCutcheon as Jessica
Hugh Grant as The Ex- Prime Minister
The little boy who grew up to be in Game of Thrones as Sam
A comic actor playing Colin, the lovably idiotic working class caterer
And also featuring a hot American Chick who digs British Boys
playing mix music to stripper music as Sandy, the hot...
American... Chick... who... digs... British... Boys!

SCENE ONE: *Emma's posh as fuck Living Room.*

EMMA: Will you be quiet up there please my little darlings. Play but play nicely. Jesus. Right, where were we. *(she takes down an old fashioned horn, blows the dust off and bellows)* Colin! So, steaks, aubergine thingy, salsa, you've got all the stuff for the dips, also the mangetout, the prawns, langoustine, the lobsters, the fruit salad, the monkfish and salmon, the pork belly, pork loin, pork ribs and the goat. So, Colin if you could prepare those and then bring them out at 8 precisely. Use the Creamware set, but be careful, it's hand-painted and from 1805. It's worth ten thousand pounds. No nothing special really, a few nibbles with friends and my bastard ex-husband to celebrate the birth of Christ and peace on earth and goodwill to all men, except one. What? The porcelain is in the cupboards above the Aga, you have used an Aga? Great... What! Not Argos... An Aga is a cooker Colin. He's not Colin Firth. I thought he was Colin Firth.

Door bell goes

COLIN!!! Answer the door. *(to audience)* Oh bloody-buggery battleships! I bet that's bloody-buggery Liam Neeson. He's always early. I don't know how he manages it. He's got seven kids. I've got two and I'm always three hours late!

COLIN enters followed by the others.

COLIN: Madame. May I present Mr Liam Neeson and his brood.

EMMA: Hello, hello little darlings, come here, that's close enough. Hello, little boy that's grown up to be in game of thrones, your'e not as cute as you were are you? No, you're not. Hello Gina, Troy, Chris, Alan, David, Phillipa. They're upstairs in the games room, yes, yes, go on up, all of you. Where's Francine, Liam?

(LIAM shakes his head)

EMMA: Oh, God! That's awful. Not again! How long have they given her? Come here my Darling, I don't believe it.

LIAM: I know. Terminal. The news was just, you know...

EMMA: I know...

LIAM: Well, yeah, you know...

EMMA: I know...

LIAM: Well, yeah, you know.

EMMA: I know. What's that been now?

LIAM: Including Francine, five.

EMMA: You should stop marrying. You are a danger. Women drop like flies when you marry... Sorry, that just.

LIAM: No, it's fine. Fine.

EMMA: Erm, drinky? Fine. What? Whisky. Of course. Excuse me. COLIN!!!!! Ah, there you are. Could you prepare a glass of the 25 year old MacEllan for this Gentleman, and I'll have a snowball. Advocat and lemonade. Advocat? It's a bright yellow liquid, in a bottle.

LIAM: Same consistency of sperm. You can't miss it, Padawan. So, I heard you invited Alan. You two must be getting on ok now. *(Karate chops)* Let the dust settle eh?

EMMA: I'm getting on with the bastard just fine. It was good of him to accept the invitation. Never thought he would. Not after what the divorce court took from him. He was apoplectic. I thought he'd have a heart attack. But that's what you get for fucking the secretary. Bitter? Not at all. Mildy annoyed and relatively wealthy.

LIAM: Speaking of wealth, how's Hugh doing now?

EMMA: Ah yes, my brother the fleeting Prime Minister. One minute you're a hero for sticking it to America, and as soon as McDonald's threaten to leave the UK, the unwashed fatty masses have an outcry and you're out on your ear.

LIAM: It was more than that though, Google, IBM, Starbucks, Subway, quite the cabal... even ASDA.

EMMA: My point exactly. Who uses ASDA? It's not as if Fortnum's were leaving is it? He's had to cancel the American lecture tour. Hardly surprising with the death threats. God, they do so overreact, the Colonials. I gather in Macy's one has to order Freedom Tea, Freedom Muffins and a Full Freedom Breakfast now.

LIAM: Is he still with the maid, that was a bit of a scandal as well wasn't it? What's her name? Martine!

EMMA: What? Little Miss Fuck Fuck Fuckity Fuck. Yes, of course. True love apparently. Ha!

Colin returns with Drinks.

EMMA: Ah, Colin. Thanks. There you go, Liam. What took you so long?

COLIN: Well, you know. Yellow and spermy. Took me a while to find. Well, I found the yellow bottle. But I had no frame of reference for the consistency so I checked with Sandy. And then I gave her a drink to wash it down. She said it's about the same, but obviously the sperm was warmer.

EMMA: Oh!

Door bell.

EMMA: Go to the kitchen. I'll get the door.

Opens door.

EMMA: Alan! Oh, you came afterall.

ALAN: Wouldn't miss it. But if I'm not welcome.

EMMA: No, of course you are. Sorry. Seasons greetings.

ALAN: How are the children. Oh. I won't interrupt them. I have gifts. For Daniel, a ouja board and for Stephen a signed copy of the Necronomicon. And for you Joni Mitchell.

EMMA: Joni Fucking Mitchell! Alan, we were married for fifteen years. Is that the only thing you picked up about me in that time

ALAN: I thought you liked her.

EMMA: We were married for fifteen years. Is that all you picked up about me in that time? Don't bother. Come in before I shut you out for good. Through there.

ALAN: I do remember. I used to live here, you know.

EMMA: I know, and what a little treasure you are for still paying the mortgage.

Door bell

EMMA: Hello. Ah, little brother, little brother, little brother, (mime Hugh) and little miss fffff... Martine. Come on in. Drinks? Of course. COLIN!!!! The kids? They're upstairs.

SCENE TWO: Kids den.

WALTER: So what's love like?

SAM: It's horrible.

WALTER: But I thought you were in love with Joanna?

SAM: Not any more. It's over.

WALTER: But you did so much to impress her. You can't be bored. You said you'd do anything for her.

SAM: Not this. I can't do this.

WALTER: What does she want you to do? Kiss her?

SAM: No. It's what I want to do. What my body wants me to do. Why my body came up with love in the first place. It's horrible. My pure heart has been betrayed by my thingy.

WALTER: YOUR THINGY! What do you mean?

SAM: I've been having sex education lessons.

WALTER: What's....???

SAM: I'll tell you. I have Mr Richards for them.

WALTER: STINKY DICK!

SAM: Yes, Stinky Dick

SCENE THREE: School Classroom

STINKY DICK: Right. Right. Settle down... Right. Where did we get to last time. Surely one of you were paying attention. What was that Smith? Cock into muff. Yes, well. We covered colloquialisms last time. Correct terms from now on please. So we continue. The penis has entered the vagina, once there, the man, I don't know... wiggles it. Jiggles it. You'll find the motion natural. Don't have to think about it really. If you're lucky she'll be on top anyway. Anyway, then the female fakes her orgasm and the male ejaculates. Which is the beginning of the end really. Marriage, in-laws, children, fees. End of desires, end of dreams.

Sorry, we'll just stick with the biology. The male ejaculate is made up of sperm. The journey of the spermatozoa. Are any of you aware of the carnage that resulted in your birth? Your Father's pumped between 100 and 300 million sperm into your mother's... into your mother's... vagina. POPULATION QUESTION: Now, half, half of those sperms died because the waters of the vagina are too acidic. What does Acid do,

Smith? That's right. Burns, Sir. So, up to a 150 million of them died, burning, screaming, praying in the waters of the vagina. Have you seen Saving Private Ryan? Good, well your Mother's vagina is Dunkirk. A seething bloody battlefield, water blood red, sperms screaming, crawling over the remnants of their dead and dying comrades. By the time they get to the egg, there are thirty left, 30! And out of those thirty, just one will reach the egg. In your case Smith, a wasted journey. Parker? How many people were killed in the last one hundred years through Genocides? That's right. 100 million. 100 million in 100 years. Think on this boys, every time you have sex the vagina is worse than Hitler, Stalin and Mussolini combined. Class dismissed.

Back to the bedroom

WALTER: And that's sex???

SAM: Yes. (pause). I'm thinking of giving homosexuality a try.

WALTER: Oh, you should. It's terribly good fun. I'm Wrigglesworths fag, you know.

SAM: Are you really?

SCENE FOUR: The kitchen

COLIN: God. The way she carries on. She's honestly expecting me to tug my forelock. If it wasn't double time Sandy I'd... pass the prawns.

SANDY: Yes you would Colin. Even if it was half time. Colin, you know, I've been here for three years and I haven't even met the Queen. Salt please.

COLIN: Neither have I. Goats eye please.

SANDY: That's the point. You never make any effort. I'm tired of being, what's the word you taught me last week?

COLIN: Rimjob?

SANDY: No, the other one. It means being poor.

COLIN: Skint? Langoustines, please.

SANDY: That's it! I'm sick of being skint and not meeting the Queen. Parsley and mint.

COLIN: Well, One, we're being paid at the end of the night, two, not quite the Queen but the old Prime Minister's here. *(kisses her)*

SANDY: Really??? Wow! Neat! Which one?

COLIN: erm...Hugh Grant.

SANDY: Oh, the one that hates us yanks! Brilliant, Colin! Pass me the freedom Muffins.

SCENE FIVE: Lounge.

MARTINE: When's dinner, I'm fucking starving?

HUGH: Er...er...er...er..er..er...er..well....er you really must try to curb that deliciously disgusting tongue of yours my dear.

MARTINE: You love my filthy tongue. You did last night and don't you deny it.

HUGH: *(His hands cover his bum, remembering where her tongue went)* Er...er....er....er...gosh. Darling, you really... Ah Liam. How are you doing? How's your lovely wife?

Reacts

HUGH: Good Lord. Really. Gosh. Five down and not out, eh? Sorry, that... er... oh bugger.

LIAM: No it's fine. How are you getting on, eh? Must be a different world, eh? No longer treading the carpeted corridors of power. Tell me, was it fucking with the Americans or fucking the maid that got you fired?

HUGH: Well...er... bit of both really.

LIAM: Up too much now?

HUGH: Not really. It didn't pan out. You see, after being Prime Minister, you usually get to join up various executive boards, get paid handsomely by the captains or kapitans of industry so they can use your address book and wheel you out at functions, look at Tony Blair. Blimey, 2 million a year for JP MORGAN, he's earned SIXTY million since he left Parliament, but I rather bollocksed all that up. Kicked out of post and party. I gather they're not even going to make me a Lord.

LIAM: Bastards! What are you doing for money?

HUGH: Ah, well, the pensions pretty reasonable. Although I was in post for less than a year, they assume that, no matter how long you do the job for, you did it for life, and were paying in from the age of sixteen. So, I'll get quite a bit in a few years. I'm borrowing against that. And writing the memoirs of course. Got an advance for that.

LIAM: Much?

HUGH: Not worth using the overseas account.

LIAM: Well, don't let them grind you down, you've got the love of a beautiful, young, healthy woman to sustain you. You'll be back on your feet in no time at all.

SANDY: Ladies and Gentlemen, Dinner is prepared! *(she sees ALAN)* OH MY GOD!!! Colin, Colin, you serve dinner, you have to. I'll... I'll be in the kitchen. Just do it!!!

SCENE NINE: After food.

EMMA: Right Gentlemen, If you'd like to follow Colin through to the Study. Brandy and Cigars will be waiting. We'll stay here.

MARTINE: What the bleeding 'ell's this, Dickens?!

EMMA: Tradition, my Dear. Colin, lead them through

COLIN offers the Gentlemen Brandy and Cigars, tugging his forelock to each. He pockets the rest and leaves.

ALAN: Nice meal. Yes Lovely. I know she's your sister Hugh, but Gentlemen, I've got to tell you it's good to be free. Like a rat that finds himself running through the streets instead of cooped up in a sterile maze... Love Rat, Hugh? very funny, a-ha! But, marriage is like a maze. Oh it should be easy. Find a partner, pick a house, have children, then the cold, eternal embrace of the grave. A straight line, uncomplicated but no. No. take the house... which your sister did, Hugh, a-ha! It's where's it going to be? What are the schools like? Will Fortnum's deliver? Questions, questions. And then out go the questions, in come demands. Daddy, I want... Daddy, I want... Then out go demands, in come arguments, Mummy says... Mummy says... Mummy says you're stealing our souls. And then one day... Free. Just like that. And you get to ask the questions. Shall I dine in or out? Shall I take the new sports car out for a spin? Shall I approach that rather fruity looking blonde over there? Will she notice the duct tape? These are the good questions. Great questions!

HUGH: Isn't that being, erm, you know, er, rather selfish?

ALAN: Yes. But why not? All I seemed to do was get under everybody's feet. They all seem to be a damn sight better off without me. And I without them. I mean, I have the children every third weekend. And I'm on the end of the phone. I'm accessible. But I'm not under anybody's feet. That's the beauty of technology.

LIAM: Are you still with the Secretary?

ALAN: No. Emma made me... get rid of her. But she was just starter's orders. I'm free. Free to go into houses of ill repute where loose women have loose morals and where looser clothing still. I'm having the time of my life.

LIAM: I...I hate the idea of divorce. When I love, I love deeply and for life.

ALAN: Yes, but your wives seem to have rather short lives. You're up to number five already. You've easily got another three in you! Sorry, was that insensitive.

LIAM: No. It's fine!!!!

MARTINE: So you don't miss having a man around? I would.

EMMA: Yes and no really. I keep thinking it would be nice for the security. You know, in an old fashioned pre-feminist way, but then I think about it logically and I've got chubb locks and a good alarm. I suppose technology has answered biology. Strangely enough my dear, it's the fornication I miss.

MARTINE: You wha???

EMMA: Well, we rarely had any, I know. But it was good to know it was there. Good to know someone still... you know. The kids came along. There comes a point, my dear, when you look in the mirror and realise you're putting on as much make up as you did when you were fourteen, but this time you're covering the tracks, and the cracks of all those years. Who would want me? Now, I mean. As a girl it was stories of fairytale Princesses and handsome Prince Charmings. And playing house and dressing the dolls. And the dolls house with furniture and furnishings. Then school and textiles and cookery, prom queens and beauty pageants. For what? To catch Prince Charming and have love for forever.

But it's not forever, is it? They don't tell you that. That one day a secretary with movie star looks and nipples facing heaven will sidle in and whisk him away. They don't tell you that Prince Charming thinks with his penis and after ten years, fifteen years, he's bored of you. Bored. That's the thing that hurts. I can take arguments and fighting because at least that's passion. But bored. Sorry to carry on. I realise it's... you see... If it wasn't for the children. I'd have been bored too.

MARTINE: Fucking hell. If that's what I've got to look forward to I can't wait. No, I mean it. Men are animals, pigs. Not your brother. He's lovely in his ditzy way. But the others. You can feel their eyes molest you. If you're lucky. Sometimes, it's more than their eyes. Just because I've made the effort to look nice, they think it's for them. It's not. It's for me. If you've got to look, don't touch. But preferably, don't fucking look!

EMMA: Doesn't Hugh say something?

MARTINE: What would Hugh be doing on a fucking bus! No, I mean when I go to work.

EMMA: You wo..wo..wo...I mean, you're gainfully employed?

MARTINE: Course.

EMMA: Well, doesn't Hugh provide for you?

MARTINE: It's not the bleeding 1890's. I pay me way. I'm not living out of his pockets. Anyway... that proves it's love. Well look. I work. I've got a job, friends and my own life. I could leave him any time I wanted to. No problem at all. Support myself? Piece of piss. Thing is, I don't want to leave him. That's what proves it's love.

SCENE ELEVEN: STUDY

ALAN: Well, you seem to be the resident expert, Mr Neeson, why don't you tell us about love.

LIAM: Love is the deepest purest emotion. I can't help falling in love. I guess I'm just a romantic at heart. Julie, my first wife, heart of gold. My Delilah. I had to take her son on, Sam of course. But love goes beyond blood. I loved him as my own. But Julie? What can I say about her without sounding pathetic or pedantic, I know I can go on. The way her hair curled, or her lips, her smile. The way she knew that the end was coming and how she dealt with it. Her eyes. True love is in the eyes. During those last months, when she couldn't get out, she needed me. Not wanted. Needed. That's love. I tended to her every need. Four month she lingered. Steadily getting weaker. Ah, those eyes.What? Oh, a rare form of botulism.

Then there was Claudia. Oh my. Her eyes. I inherited little Gina from her. She lasted five months after it struck. What? Oh, botulism again.

Then Barbara, remember Barbie? So vivacious, so full of life. Gone in two months. I expected her to last longer somehow. But she left me Troy and Chris. Hmm? E-coli.

HUGH: Where on earth were you eating?

LIAM: Oh, home. We always do. I'm a bit of a whiz in the kitchen.

HUGH: And you didn't get ill?

LIAM: No

HUGH: Never? And the children?

LIAM: No. And now Francine. Who knows how long she'll go on. But those eyes. The same with all my beautiful women. It's a wonderful feeling to be needed. Especially by a woman you love. Of course, she's going to leave me with Alan, David and Phillipa. Seven children. I sure didn't plan on that. I think a couple are going to have to go this year.

ALAN: Have you ever heard of Munchausen by proxy?

LIAM: Pure love.

SCENE TWELVE: Kitchen

SANDY: Colin, I've got to tell you something. Sit down. You remember when I said I worked in Sales. That's how I raised the money for this business.

COLIN: Yes.

SANDY: Well, it wasn't strictly sales. It was... Oh Jesus. It was... I was a stripper.

COLIN: When?

SANDY: Shortly after I got here. I did it before in the States. To pay my way through college. I wasn't the only one. Lots of college girls did it. A few of them did porno as well. I never did. The money was real good but... I just needed my degree, you know. You guys don't realise how lucky you are to have grants.

COLIN: We don't anymore.

SANDY: Well, at least you've got the NHS and Welfare. You guys are so...civilised. It's like, that's the highest we've reached. The high water mark in the bath of society.

COLIN: Yes, but, some people are pretty determined to pull the plug out. I mean, I read that two thirds of the cabinet are worth 60 million quid between them. And that 60% of MP's are millionaires. They don't use the NHS. No need to. But my Gran does, I do. Our kids'll have too. Especially if I keep on earning this. When were you stripping?

SANDY: After a month of London. It's expensive here. I finished two months ago. I earned enough to give this a go with you. It was just for the money. Lots of the girls are on drugs, that's where their money goes. Not me though. They also hang around the club on days off, meeting the customers out of hours. You know.

COLIN: I... Did you? You know... Sleep with any of your clientele.

SANDY: No. Never. No matter how much they offered.

COLIN: How much did they...

SANDY: Anything between 500 and a thousand usually.

COLIN: Dollars?

SANDY: Pounds. Except one guy. He wouldn't take no for an answer.

COLIN: He didn't...

SANDY: No. We have very big men to make sure that never happens. No. He just kept upping the price. One thousand, two, three four.

COLIN: Four grand?

SANDY: He got up to eight. What makes people think they can buy anything they want. Even people. I told him, I ain't a whore. He... laughed in my face. I can't be bought. I love you Colin. I'm sorry.

COLIN: Hey, hey, don't cry. You didn't sleep with him. Sod him. I would've for eight thousand. Five hundred would've turned my head. I don't care.

SANDY: I wanted to tell you, but I was ashamed.

COLIN: Hey, you were earning money. For us. I don't care that you stripped. You could've been a prostitute for all I care. You could have a thousand ex-boyfriends. What business is it of mine. I love you. So, you took off your clothes. I love girls that take off their clothes. I mean. Look. I love you.

SANDY: I hate places like this. They've got all the money and none of the worry. How much is that stove worth? And the dinner service? Did she ever get her tits out to pay for it? Will they ever use the NHS? Colin, are we always going to be servants?

COLIN: Look, relax. We're not servants. We're caterers. Just...

EMMA: *(offstage)* COLIN!!!

COLIN: I'll fix the drinks. You stay here.

Undoes his fly.

SCENE THIRTEEN: Lounge

COLIN: A Jug of Snowballs for everyone. Fill your glasses ladies and gents. Madam? Sir? Madam? Sir? Sir?

ALAN: Snowball?

COLIN: Drink of the season Sir. It's in the name. Felicitations. Congratulations and warm wishes. Has everyone finished with the dishes? I'll tidy and collate them madam.

EMMA: Please do. And be careful. Ten thousand pounds.

COLIN: I shall Madame. Sandy shall serve the Sherry.

EMMA: Well, cheers everyone. I hope you have a marvellous Christmas. The season of goodwill. Cheers.

They all drink

SANDY: It's you.

ALAN: Hello Loretta. What are you... oh, catering. You're a caterer now. Moving up in the world.

SANDY: Just along, Sir.

EMMA: Loretta, this is Sandy.

ALAN: Sorry, terrible with names, Sandy. Where did we meet?

SANDY: The titty bar in shoreditch. You must remember, you offered me a lot of money to sleep with you.

EMMA: You dirty piece of shit. And you? A whore?

ALAN: Now, now. Harmless fun.

EMMA: Sod off, Alan. And you, get out of my house. Get out.

COLIN: What's going on?

SANDY: He's the eight grand man.

Colin punches out Alan

COLIN: Not everything is for sale.

EMMA: Get out, you oick. Alan, darling, speak to me. Don't think you're getting paid.

COLIN: That's fine. Hope you enjoyed the snowballs. Not so much advocat in that batch, but definitely the consistency of sperm. Ta-ta.

COLIN: *(Addresses audience)* And me and Sandy left. Taking the dinner service of course. Now, me jizzing in the Snowballs was pretty immature, infantile, and if Richard Curtis had written this, he'd have had me do it because I'm a working class idiot, an oick, a chav. Yeah, I can't remember one sympathetic working class character he's done. Baldric? Rhys Ifans in Notting Hill,

Me in Love Actually? Martine in Love Actually, no, that was just patronising. Yeah, none of them. But Richard Curtis didn't write this. And I jizzed in the Snowballs for a completely different reason.

The UN released an equality report which said the UK's wealth inequality, percentage-wise, is the same as one other country. Anyone guess? Nigeria. The top five families in this country own the equivalent of the bottom twelve and a half million people, twenty percent of the country. Before the Second World War the top 0.1% earned a hundred and forty times the average working wage, not the lowest, the average. Then came the Second World War and the creation of the welfare state, and through the re-distrbution of wealth that figure dropped, till it reached its lowest point in the 70's, which was twenty times the national average wage. Then came Thatcher, followed by Major, Blair and this cunt. And that figure rose and rose until it's now... yeah, back to a hundred and forty times the national average, and climbing faster and higher.

I jizzed in the snowballs because all over this world, it's rich against poor and you've got to help out in anyway you can.

Goodnight!

SOUND – *Pissing In The Wine* by Chumbawamba

PART SEVEN

300 to 1

First performed at the Banshee Labyrinth Chamber Room as part of the PBH Free Fringe 2014. Directed by Gareth Armstrong. Developed with public funds via Arts Council England and support from The Stephen Joseph Theatre, Scarborough.

V.O: 300 to 1, Featuring Leonidas, King of Sparta, Xerxes, the Persian God-King And YOU as 300 spartan warriors with taught, tight bodies and asses to die for.
Also featuring Wilfred Owen, the First World War poet.
And Siegfried Sasson, Another First World War poet
And featuring as Ephialtes the traitor, Lawrence Olivier as Richard III
And also starring... Tim. A 15 year old boy.

Audience, do you accept a 41 year old man can play a boy? Honestly, the show can't go on unless you shout yes... Good! Engage the suspension of disbelief!

(Softer voice)
Now meet Tim, a boy whose hormones are vibrating so hard, he can only temper his testosterone fuelled anger by thinking about the English Teacher, Mrs Henderson's, Breasts. He has just run all the way home to his bedroom...

TIM: *(Launches school bag onto stage)* Bloody Homework! *(to audience)* I hate School, hate it! *(pause)* But you need an Education nowadays. You really do. Everybody has degrees now, everybody – even Mr Jones, school caretaker... he has a 2:1, from Aberystwyth.

Anyway, Homey homework..War poetry. *(Studies book)* Well that's good and bad. War... I mean that's Good, exciting. Have you heard of hellfire missiles? Helicopter Launch FIRE and forget! They can take out a baddie even if he's on a motorbike. *(mimes missile launch and motorcycle hit)* BOOM! Amazing... and then there's Poetry and that's just... Bobbins! I mean, why would you even write a poem when you're in the middle of a war? I mean, really? There's Bombs dropping. Machine guns and no man's land. And there's tanks, and you've never seen these before, like Huge steel houses rolling over towns and trenches. Do you really think "OOOOH, the Clouds are nice today, OOOH, the daffodils have come up. Where's me pen, I feel a poem coming on." Seriously?

(Looks at book.) War poetry. "For the fallen", sounds cheerful. "Before Action", that one sounds quite good! "In flanders fields", "Here dead we lie." Look at this one...It's not even in English! Dulchy et Decorum Est Pro....Who wrote this rubbish?!

WILFRED OWEN: *(Appearing with a whoosh from the ether. To audience)* Do you mean Dulce Decorum Est Pro Patria Mori? *(to TIM)* I did actually. *(To audience)* Wilfred Owen. 1893 – 1918.

TIM: What the fu... fudge does it mean?

WILF; It's from Horace. Latin... "It is sweet and fitting to die for your country". Don't you study Latin? But it's the gateway to the Romance Languages! Once you've learnt that, Spanish, French, Italian, they open up like little flowers. Why don't they teach you it? Oh, sorry, are you a bit of a dunce?

TIM: No, I'm top of the class, top of the year! I get bullied between every lesson to prove it. I don't know why they don't teach us it.

WILF: Neither do I, like hamstringing a horse and expecting it to run in the Derby!

TIM: Why did you write poetry in the War? I mean, you were in the middle of a war? The Great War.

WILF: Trust me young man, it wasn't that great. I got killed a week before the thing ended. Did you know the Generals had all agreed on peace, and then they waited, and waited, and waited so they could finish on the 11th hour of the 11th day of the 11th month. Do you know how many men died for a palindromic poster? But, The poetry was down to Siegfried... Sassoon? No? What do they teach you? He was the "most beautiful, most superb, most masculine poet" in the world. I met him in the Hospital...

FLASHBACK (Moves forward)

SIEGFRIED SASSOON: Hello Old Boy, Siegfried.

WILF: Wilfred. *(Hand out for shake)*

SIEG: *(Ignores)* Fritz ding you, did he?

WILF: Yes. You?

SIEG: No, Shell shock. But I'll soon be back with my lovely lads. Bringing up the rear. We're joined at the hips, you know.

WILF: Erm, what are the Nurses like here?

SIEG: Gorgeous to a man.

WILF: You're Sassoon the poet?

SIEG: Yes. Sassoon the hairdresser won't be along for another fifty years.

WILF: I love your work.

SIEG: Thank you. It's not been easy, Poeting for King and Country. No picnic keeping the populace's pecker up. Loins girded. Lip stiff. To be honest, it's hard and getting harder. I have a creeping suspicion that the chaps at HQ don't have a clue what's going on down here.

WILF: Crikey! Isn't that a bit....

SIEG: Controversial?

WILF: Well, more blasphemous!

SIEG: Maybe, old fruit. But look here love, I stuff my boys regularly with pluck, and those plucky fellows come back damaged.

WILF: They run out of pluck?

SIEG: They're plucking dead, old love. And the chaps at the chessboard just call it one-all. If they notice at all.

WILF: We should do something!

SIEG: Well, I am old fruit. It's a bit hush-hush.

WILF: What are you going to do?

SIEG: I'm... Come here... I'm... *(whispers)*

WILF: You're what!

SIEG: Yes, radical times call for radical action. But keep it schtum, Wilfred. Loose lips, Old boy, eh!

WILF: You... you... you're *(shouts)* you're going to write a poem!

SIEG: Shhhhh! Yes! That'll show 'em.

WILF: *(Eager)* I could help you, I've written one or two...

SIEG: Can you rhyme? Absolutely essential in a poem that, Wilfred.

WILF: Well... not so much.

SIEG: Listen Wilfred, I like you. You've got the right sort of spunk for a job like this. I'll teach you. *(Arm around Owen)* Old love, you're going to Sweat your guts out writing poetry and we're going to change the world!

FLASHBACK OVER

WILF: So that was that. We told the Old HQ what was what. And Poetry saved the day.

TIM: Dulce et Decorum Est Pro Patria Mori?

WILF: *(sarcastic)* It is sweet and fitting to die for your country

TIM: Exactly! Thanks Wilfred.

WILF: What?

TIM: You've made up my mind for me.

WILF: What?

TIM: I'm joining the army. It is sweet and fitting to die for your country. You wrote that!

WILF: *(Worried)* Yes... Erm, young man, I think you may have grabbed the wrong end of my stick.

TIM: It's the only solution, the only one that makes any real, common sense. Look, I need to be educated.

WILF: I can't argue with you there.

TIM: I can't afford to go to Uni, I'll be in debt till I'm 60, mum and dad won't let me... But, if I join up, the Army pays for my education. No debt. No loans. And one educated, graduated fellow. Plus the army'll make a man of me. No more bullying.

WILF: I'm not sure that's how it works.

TIM: *(Ignoring)* Plus, if the worse thing that can happen is to die in glory on the battlefield, get my name read out in the Houses of Parliament and have stories spun about me from now until the end of time, it's a win-win. Just like 300!

WILF: 300?

TIM: Yeah, 300. The film, 300! 300!

WILF: Will you stop saying that! 300 What?

TIM: The 300 Spartans!

WILF: Oh... do you mean the battle of Thermopylae from the second Persian invasion of Greece led by Xerxes son of Darius in the autumn of 480 BC passed down to us from the Histories of Herodotus?

TIM: Do I? I think I do. Yes. Look, there's this King...

WILF: *(Goes to fetch Siegfried)* Siegfried! Are you still here? Come back!

SIEG: Hello, old boy. What's all the fuss?

WILF: *(Moves chair)* Take a seat. We're about to be entertained.

SIEG: Oh really, what with?

WILF: The three hundred spartans!

SIEG: Oh, you mean the battle of Thermopylae from...

WILF: Yes yes, shh!

SIEG: Excellent. Let's have a proper gander at the propaganda, so to speak.

WILF: Young man, pray continue.

TIM: Right, there's this King. Leonidas. And He's tall, dark, his eyes glint in the Greek sun like cold blue steel, his beard manly. Muscles taut, his chest broad, legs smooth, wearing only tight leather shorts girding his loins. His naked oily skin shining in the autumn haze...

WILF: Siegfried, it sounds a bit homo-erotic...

SIEG: Positively Gay, old boy. I must say I like idea of the uniform though, not only fetching but far superior to the itchy khaki we were trussed in.

WILF: So it is... gay, Siegfried?

SIEG: Totally Wilfred.

TIM: It's NOT gay! It can't be, he's married! He's teaching his son how to be a warrior, with the Queen, who's really fit... like Mrs Henderson in English fit... perfect breasts, when a messenger arrives.

(Imitates Messenger on rearing horse)

MONKEY POET *(to audience)* So sorry Ladies and Gentlemen, there's something missing from this part of the show and that is the Tension Music!

(Divide audience and get them to chant tension music)

MESSENGER: Greetings Leoni...

TIM: Sorry, it's a bit deeper than that...

MESS: Gree... gree... greetings Leonidas, great king! I come from the living God King Xerxes.

TIM: And the messenger dumps this bag of human heads down right at Leonidas' feet.

MESS: Great King.

LEONIDAS: Aye, y'alright? This is the wife, Gorgi. And I think you'll find she is. Before you talk, messenger. Know that everyone is responsible for what comes out their mouths, even messengers. What does Xerxes want?

MESS: Earth and water

QUEEN: Don't be coy and don't be stupid. You can afford neither.

MESS: Why can this woman talk freely in front of men?

QUEEN: Because only spartan women give birth to real men.

WILF: Kai tiktomen monai andras. She actually said that to an Athenian Lady.

SIEG: Historically accurate is it then old boy?

WILF: *(Outburst of laughter)* don't be silly, Siggy?

LEO: Let's go over to the well. Maybe some fresh water will cool our tongues. Speak.

MESS: I have come from Xerxes, who commands an army so massive, the ground shakes when it marches, it's numbers so great it drinks whole rivers dry. All he requires is a gift of Earth and Water. A token of Sparta's submission.

LEO: Submission... Word has it that the Athenian's have already turned you down, and if those philosophers and boy lovers have found that kind of backbone, and what with Spartans having their reputation to think of...

MESS: Choose your next words carefully Leonidas... they maybe your last as king.

TIM: You bring the severed heads of crowned kings to my city steps, you insult my queen, you threaten my people with slavery and death, oh I have chosen my words carefully Persian. Perhaps you should have done the same. Earth and water, you'll find plenty of both down there.

MESS: No one threatens a messenger. This is blasphemy. Madness

TIM: The King looks at the people under his protection, he sees a child suckling at its mothers breast. *(Double take)* And his queen.

Queen nods with throat slitting gesture

LEO: Madness? Madness?

MP: MUSIC PLEASE!

LEO: THIS IS MANCHESTER! I mean SPARTA

(Slow motion kicks. Get audience to do slow screams – fall to seat.)

WILF: Manchester, eh? Are we in Manchester??

TIM: Yes, Well, Sparta, Manchester. It's pretty much the same thing, eh? Have you seen our football teams? And the supporters... City and United, that's Sparta. And the women, Manchester women... like Mrs Henderson and her perfect...

SIEG: And if you march to a different drum, there's the village on Canal Street, capital of gay culture. Oh you must Wilfred, even as a ghost.

WILF: *(Ignoring Siggy)* Erm... Manchester! I served with the Manchester Regiment, young man! Write that down in your homework. Bound to get an extra couple of marks there, Wilfred Owen, erstwhile Manchester regiment.

SIEG: Not very sporting to kick a messenger down a well, though is it, Wilfred. Not even Fritz would do that!

WILF: I agree Siegfried. One simply doesn't shoot the messenger. However, back to Dulce Decorum est... The messenger died for his country. Was that sweet and fitting?

TIM: Well, no, you've got to wait for the sweet and fitting deaths, They're near the end to be honest. But right, the next thing Leonidas has to do, is climb a mountain to the temple of the Ephors, the priests, to ask for permission to go to war.

WILF: He's not even got permission to go to war and he threw the messenger down the Well!

SIEG: I used to have to ask permission to go to the lavatory... great fun.

TIM: And these Ephors, like all priests and some celebrities from the 70's are horrible perverts... *(imitates)*

WILF: Hold on, I was going to be a priest!

SIEG: Really old boy, why?

WILF: Many reasons... some of the music is particularly uplifting... erm... the architecture is quite... erm...

SIEG: Ah, come on Wilfred

WILF: I found the chastity of the clergy appealing...

SIEG: That's cos you were really a bender, old boy. Write that down in your homework, Wilfred Owen was gay. Definitely worth a couple of marks. You don't mind do you, Wilfred?

WILF: *(Squeaks)* No. Of course. Erm. My orientation, though private, should be...can be...discussed in a child's homework...

SIEG: You see, Wilfred here is what we call a repressed homosexual. Now, I was not openly homosexual, but blatantly homosexual. One of the advantages of being stinking rich. My parents and I knew from the day I was born, after all they called me Siegfried Lorraine Sassoon.

WILF: Some do. For others... feelings develop over time... that are hard to reconcile with other's expectations and your own expectations.

TIM: OK. PRIDE meeting over! The King climbs the mountain. The Ephors, the priests are waiting...

EPHOR: Hello Leonidas, we've been expecting you. Come in, speak.

LEO: The Persians claim their forces number in the millions. They may exaggerate. But there's no doubt we face the most massive army ever assembled. We will use our superior fighting skills and the terrain of Greece herself. We will rebuild the sea wall funnelling the Persians into the pass we call (get magazine, opens at topless page) The Hot Gates! Xerxes numbers will count for nothing in that tight pass. Wave upon wave of Persians will attack and smash themselves on Spartan shields and none shall pass, Xerxes men shall become so demoralized, their losses so great, that they shall have no choice but to abandon their campaign.

EPHOR: First we must ask the Oracle Leonidas.

TIM: The Ephors only have the most beautiful girls in Sparta to be the oracle and they dance to divine the future, like this *(dances with magazine and licks page)*

EPHOR: She says Put your faith in the old god's Leonidas. The Carneia. The army cannot march.

LEO: If I put my faith in the old gods, then Sparta will burn and her daughters become slaves or worse... Please? Please? Fine foul priest.

EPHOR: Then we cut to the Kings bedchamber. Leonidas is naked. Looking out over the city. (strips shows arse, pause) IT'S NOT GAY! And the Queen is in the bedchamber and she's naked, and she's fit, like Mrs Henderson fit... (MIME) He strokes a hair from her face... touches her ear... strokes down her neck. To her shoulder. He brings his hand down, around the curve of her breast and towards the raised coloured skin of the nip...

SIEG: I think we can skip this bit.

TIM: WHAT! NO! This is Mrs Henderson, I mean the Queen. Please. I want to carry on the scene!

SIEG: Course you do, you're 15

WILF: There's nothing wrong with abstinence, young man. Take Cold showers, go for a run. Sleep with your boxing gloves on.

TIM: Right. Right!

Next Scene. Daybreak. Leonidas goes to the field outside the city walls where his men await.

LEO: Ah, captain. The men are ready?

CAPTAIN: All 300 sire.

LEO: All have sons?

CAPTAIN: All Sire.

LEO: Captain, him? That's your son. He's not old enough to have lain with a woman.

TIM: *(Pointedly at WILF)* I know how he feels!

CAPTAIN: Sire, he's no younger than we were the first time and I have two others.

LEO: A good friend you are...but Captain, there is none better...

EPHOR: (Running in) Sire! Sire! The army are forbidden to march.

LEO: So they are. I'm feeling a bit stiff. Decided to stretch my legs, take a stroll...This is my personal guard.

EPHOR: Take a stroll....Where... whereabouts may I ask?

LEO: Now you mention it, thought I might go up North.

EPHOR: The Hot Gates!

LEO: Aye. This is Goodbye, Priest.

QUEEN: My husband! Spartan!

LEO: Yes My Lady

QUEEN: Come back with your shield...or on it.

WILF: Air tan air epitas That was a saying of spartan women.

SIEG: Yes, I knew a few Generals with that attitude. Well anyone who wasn't going to the front

TIM: Goodbye, my love... He doesn't say it because there is no room for softness, not in Sparta no place for weakness, only the hard and strong may call themselves Spartans only the hard, only the strong.

WILF: It's really not healthy for young men to contain all that emotion.

SIEG: They can't all be poets, old love.

TIM: So we marched... and marched... and marched... and marched... and marched. There was lots of marching in 480 BC.

SIEG: Really! There was lots of marching in 1914!

WILF: *(Reading from war poetry book)*

And towards our distant rest began to trudge.
Men marched asleep. Many had lost their boots
But limped on, blood-shod. All went lame; all blind;
Drunk with fatigue;

TIM: Yeah, grim! But this is Greece, it's sunny you know. I saw it on a holiday show.

LEO: Daxos and the Arcadians! A pleasant surprise!

DAXOS: The morning is full of surprises Leonidas. We were told Sparta was on the warpath. We were eager to join forces. But you bring this handful (indicates audience) against Xerxes. We expected Sparta's commitment to at least equal our own.

LEO: Doesn't it? You there, Arcadian, what is your profession?

ARCADIAN 1: I am a potter sir.

LEO: And you Arcadian. Your profession?

ARC 2: A baker, sir.
LEO: And you?

ARC 3: Sculptor, sir

LEO: And you?

ARC 4: I just call the bingo

MP: And now for those of you who haven't seen the film, there's a bit of call and response. Leonidas is going to say "Spartans – what's your profession?" and you all reply AWOO! AWOO! Got that? Quick practice. *(Does)* Good!

LEO: Spartans, What's your profession?

AUDIENCE: AWOO! AWOO!

LEO: You see old friend, I brought more soldiers than you.

TIM: And the march leads us to...

LEO: The Hot Gates! How's the seawall coming along?

CAPTAIN: Finished it sire

LEONIDAS: Excellent. Captain, Have the men found any route over the hills to our backs because that would be pretty awful strategically?

CAPTAIN: None Sire

EPHIALTES (LAURENCE OLIVIER as RICHARD 3rd): There is such a route sire. The Persians could use it to outflank us.

CAPTAIN: Silence monster or I'll skewer you where you stand

LEO: I gave no such order. Leave us. Forgive the Captain, a good soldier but short on manners.

EPHIALTES: There' nothing to forgive. I know what I look like. I am Ephialtes, born of Sparta, my mothers love led my parents to flee, lest I be discarded.
WILF: The Spartans practiced infanticide. Really beastly to their boys.

SIEG: Sounds like my old school, Marlborough

144

WILF: Disabled children were cast out to survive as best they could.

SIEG: Sounds like the current Government's policy

EPHIALTES: My father taught me the Spartan way. Allow me to serve you great king and redeem my father's name. I will kill many Persians. My arms are strong, my thrust is long...

SIEG: Remember when said about rhymes Wilfred?

WILF: Yes siggy?

SIEG: That's a bad one.

LEO: A fine thrust, but... raise your shield as high as you can? (EPHIALTES does) Your father should have taught you how a phalanx works. We fight as a single impenetrable unit. That's the source of our strength. Each Spartan protects the man to the left of him from thigh to neck with his shield. Any weak spot and the phalanx shatters. From thigh to neck. You can't hold your shield high enough. I'm sorry, Ephialtes. I cannot use you.

LEO exits

EPHIALTES: Noooooooooo! You were wrong father! You were wrong mother. You are wrong Leonidas!

(ground shakes)

MP: *(To audience)* TENSION MUSIC PLEASE! Could you stamp your feet as well please?

CAPTAIN: What's that, Sire? Is it an Earthquake?

LEO: That's no earthquake. Persians! Thousands of them!

WILF: Yes Siggy, we think there were between 70 and 300 thousand Persians at Thermopylae.

SIEG: Twice as many men died at Passchendaele. 600 thousand men, or the Somme, 50,000 casualties on the first day. "People read that life on the front line was Hell, how could they know what that one word, hell, means?" Wilfred... (passes book, the following, including the previous Hell quote are taken from anonymous French soldiers who served at Verdun)

WILF: "Men were squashed. Cut in two or divided from top to bottom. Blown into showers; bellies turned inside out; skulls forced into the chest as if by a blow from a club."

(Past tense – ate, drank etc)

"You eat beside the dead; you drink beside the dead, you relieve yourself beside the dead and you sleep beside the dead"

(To self)

To die from a bullet (like I did) seems to be nothing; parts of our being remain intact; but to be dismembered, torn to pieces, reduced to pulp...

TIM: Bloody hell fellas, cheer up! Let's get back to the story. The Persian captain rides over to the hot gates, where the Greeks and Spartans are gathered in the crevasse in the mountains.

PERSIAN: Spartans. Lay down your weapons!

(A spear is chucked killing the Persian dead.)

WILF: Dulce decorum est, young man? All he said was lay down your arms?

SIEG: Was that sweet and fitting?

TIM: Oh shut up! Leonidas replies...

LEO: Persians. Come and get them!

WILF: Molone labe. That's still the motto of the Greek Army, Siggy.
SIEG: As well as a branch of American Special Forces! Thieving Sods!

TIM: And then they FIGHT!

(Slow motion fight)

WILF: What on earth is he doing?

SIEG: Some sort of contemporary dance, I think.

TIM: It's... I'm trying to do a battle scene in slow motion. It's not easy on your own. I saw this solo show, "One-man Lord of the Rings," he did these massive battles...

WILF: One man?

SIEG: You saw a show with just one man? God how dreadful.

TIM: Shut up! There's nothing wrong with one man shows! After the first battle, there is brief respite and the Spartans go round killing the Persian wounded. *(Mimes)*.

CAPTAIN: Persians approach my lord, a small contingent, too small for an attack.

LEO: Maybe they feel like a chat. I'm on my way. Captain, you're in charge

CAPTAIN: But Sire!

LEO: Relax. If they kill me, all of Sparta goes to war. Pray they're that stupid. Pray we're that lucky. Besides, there's no reason we can't be civil, is there.

CAPTAIN: (Kills Persian) None sire.

TIM: Leonidas goes to the beach and sees a throne gliding across the sand towards him, carried by a hundred slaves. And on it, Xerxes, The living god king. And he's about 8 foot tall. With piercings all over his body. And chains. And he wears this golden codpiece.

LEO: How do, bonnie lad? Let me guess, you would be Xerxes?

XERXES: Leonidas, it would be nothing short of madness if you and your valiant troops were perish all because of a regrettable misunderstanding. Consider the beautiful land you so vigorously defend, imagine it reduced to ash. Consider the fate of your women.

LEO: You don't know our women. I may as well have marched them up here judging from what I have seen. You have many men, but, few soldiers. It wont be long before they fear my spears more than your whips.

XERXES: It's not the lash they fear but my divine power. But I am a generous god. I can make you rich beyond measure. I will make you warlord of Greece. Your Athenian rivals will kneel at your feet, if you but kneel at mine.

LEO: That's quite an offer, I'd be crazy to refuse it. But this kneeling business. I'm afraid killing all those slaves of yours has left me with a nasty cramp in my leg. I think I'll walk it off.

XERXES: As generous as I am I can be cruel. I will erase Sparta from the histories. There will be no glory in your sacrifice. No one will ever know

LEO: They'll know that Free men stood against a tyrant, that a band of brothers died standing against a far larger force, and by the end of this, they'll know that even a god can bleed.

TIM: And Xerxes goes Batshit crazy. He sends in Rhinos, Elephants, tribes who have discovered gunpowder and grenades and I don't know how because it's 480 BC but it's in the film so it must be true. And nothing breaks down the Spartan reserve till... the traitor!!

XERXES: The Gods were cruel to shape you so, Ephialtes, and the Spartans cruel to reject you. Here we have, nymphs from a thousand kingdoms. Where are you from my dear?
WOMAN: Numidia, my Lord.

XERXES: Very nice. Lead my men to the hidden path behind the cursed Spartans and you can have it all, your joys will be endless.

EPHIALTES: I want it all, women, land, wealth, and one thing more... a uniform.

XERXES: It's yours.

LEO: Daxos!

DAXOS: Leonidas, we are undone. A hunchback traitor has led Xerxe's men to the hidden path. By the morning we will be surrounded. The Hot Gates will fall.

LEO: Good. Spartans prepare for GLORY!

DAXOS: Are you mad? There's no glory to be had now. Only retreat, or surrender, or death.

LEO: That's an easy choice for us Arcadian, Spartans never retreat, Spartans never surrender, go, spread the word. Let every Greek search his soul, and whilst you're at it, search your own. Men, tomorrow we light a fire that will burn in the hearts of free men down the centuries. A new age is begun. An age of reason, an age of justice, an age of liberty, an age of law, an age of freedom. And all will know that 300 Spartans gave their last breath to defend it. They may take our lives but they'll never take our FREEDOM! Tartans... I mean, Spartans, ready your breakfast, for tonight we dine in hell!

TIM: The Persians find the Spartans defended, shields surrounding them like a tortoise shell. Leonidas stands in front of his men like this. Xerxes approaches on his throne. A Persian spokesman steps forward, next to him is Ephialtes the traitor in his new uniform.
SPOKESMAN: My compliments Leonidas... and my congratulations. You have surely turned calamity into victory. Despite your arrogance, the god king has come to admire Spartan fighting skill and valour. You fight for your kingship? You will be made warlord of all Greece. Just drop your arms and kneel to one true master of the world.

EPHIALTES: Yield Leonidas, use your reason. Think of your men.

LEO: *(Takes off helmet)* You, Ephialtes, May you live forever.

EPHIALTES: Nooooo!

SIEG: If anyone offered me unlimited wealth, men, power, and the chance to live forever with it, I'd take it.

WILF: It would mean betraying your country, Siggy.

SIEG: They said I practically did that anyway. That's why I was in the Hospital when I met you dear boy. Shell shock! All I did was write an open letter questioning HQ's policy. They decided I must be mad and had me committed. People are like that when you don't toe their line.

TIM: Shhhh! This is the moment.

MP: Ladies and Gents, for the last time in this show, please... Tension Music!

(Slow motion)

LEO: NOW!

TIM: The Spartans split from their formation. Someone passes Leonidas a spear. Leonidas throws his spear, *(mimes)* and the living god king bleeds!

MP: And then all 300 die. *(To audience)* C'mon then! Your best heroic dying please! And one Spartan warrior crawls to the king and touches his hand.

SPARTAN: It was an honour to die at your side sire

LEO: And it was an honour to live at yours.

(The Men grip arms as they die. Pause as we take in the scene.)

TIM: *(Glances at Wilfred and Siegfried)* LOOK HOLDING HANDS ISN'T GAY!

So you see, It is sweet and fitting to die for your country. Cos Leonidas fought for freedom and freedom isn't free. It comes with the highest cost of all. The blood and sacrifice of young men and women everywhere. "Go tell the Spartans, stranger passing by, that here obedient to Spartan law, we die."

SIEG: God, that rhyme is awful... Wilfred learnt a thing or two from me you know, read this one.

TIM: *(Reading Dulce et Decorum Est Pro Patria Mori by Wilfred Owen)*
Bent double, like old beggars under sacks,
Knock-kneed, coughing like hags, we cursed through sludge,
Till on the haunting flares we turned our backs,
And towards our distant rest began to trudge.
Men marched asleep. Many had lost their boots,
But limped on, blood-shod. All went lame; all blind;
Drunk with fatigue; deaf even to the hoots
Of gas-shells dropping softly behind.

Gas! GAS! Quick, boys!—An ecstasy of fumbling
Fitting the clumsy helmets just in time,
But someone still was yelling out and stumbling
And flound'ring like a man in fire or lime.—
Dim through the misty panes and thick green light,
As under a green sea, I saw him drowning.

In all my dreams before my helpless sight,
He plunges at me, guttering, choking, drowning.

If in some smothering dreams, you too could pace
Behind the wagon that we flung him in,
And watch the white eyes writhing in his face,
His hanging face, like a devil's sick of sin;
If you could hear, at every jolt, the blood
Come gargling from the froth-corrupted lungs,
Obscene as cancer, bitter as the cud
Of vile, incurable sores on innocent tongues,—
My friend, you would not tell with such high zest
To children ardent for some desperate glory,
The old Lie: Dulce et decorum est
Pro patria mori.

SIEG: *(Picks up TIMs exercise book and starts scribbling in it, over his speech.)* Well done young man. Beautiful Wilfred. But you're both wrong. It's not the dying. Death, whether Honourable or not, glorious or not, is the end. What happens if you survive? That's was my test after the First World War. How many broken men I saw with missing arms and legs. You go out so perfect and healthy and bright... and come back... even if you come back whole, you cannot leave the battlefield behind. Shell-shock, post traumatic stress, even adjusting to the fact that no one is bellowing orders at you all day. How do you live in the quiet of civilian life?

MP: You can't. According to the charity Combat Stress, 20% of all those serving will develop mental health issues. According to Soldiers Off The Streets up to 30% of homeless people are ex-service Men and Women. In Prisons, 10% of the prison population are ex-services. We reached a horrific statistic a couple of years ago when it was revealed that more veterans of the Falklands had committed suicide that died on the battlefield, We glorify the dead. They get their names read out in the houses of commons, while the survivors, like the homeless, are walked passed and ignored. That has to change.

SIEG: So Young man, don't you fall for that old lie, Dulce et decorum est Pro patria mori. Here young man your homework is done. *(Siegfried places Tim's exercise book on the table).* C'mon Wilfred. You need to make up for lost time. I know this lovely little bar on Canal St...

(The two old soldiers and friends walk arm in arm offstage.)

Lights fade.

END

A shit-load of thanks...

First off, thanks to you for buying this book. If it was at one of my shows. Double-thanks. If it was off a shelf... Triple Thanks. Poetry books hardly fly off the shelves. In 2014 the highest selling poet, Carol Ann Duffy sold a total of £200k's worth over the year. Hardly Stephen King is it? So thanks for not letting this one gather dust with the others!

Going from being paper-shaking first time reader to full time poet/performer/producer/tour booker/director in ten years has been an eventful journey to say the least, and one that's full of coincidence and synchronicity. I have to thank the poet Mike Garry for getting up in a pub in Withington, Manchester, and reciting some poems between bands prompting my question, "Is that allowed?" and following it up with the overly bold statement "I can do that."   John G Hall and Lucia Cox for running the night *City Lights* at which, as MC, I introduced Jem Rolls, who over beers afterwards told me of the Canadian Fringe Circuit. In 2007 I boldly went to Canada with my first hour set, and have to thank Kathy Navackas of the London Fringe for being the first place to put me on. And the two awards I won there, best in venue and Producer's Pick. That tour was a delight aside from the incident in San Francisco where on opening night I had a heckle that I smoothly put down resulting in the gentlemen leaving and returning to hurl a bin full of bottles over the audience and at me. (Read all about it in *Monkey Poet's Murder Mystery* on page 81 proving that the best thing about being a writer performer is that any scary/horrible incident/experience is at least a source of good material). Thanks to Pauline Moffatt of the IndyFringe whose been a constant source of support and encouragement. Thanks to the performers who I met on the way and the conversations about performance we had, the great thing about fringes is that there's a whole mix of disciplines, for example, the clown Jonno Katz gave me a great physical gag for my show, so great that at the end of the tour in San Francisco it got the biggest laugh, but to the others, Phil Van Hest, Paul Hutcheson, Andy McQuade, who went on to direct Murder Mystery and LOVE*hurts*ACTUALLY, Alex Dallas who was so instrumental in *Welcome to the UK!* She even titled it. Jon Bonfiglio for organising the Kuiperfest festival in the Catalonian Mountains where I met the Debt records people, and the lovely Biff Roxby who produced my first album (second one's coming, honest!) Jon knew Nick Awde, the reviewer in the Stage, who came to see my show *Welcome to Afghanistan* in Edinburgh at the Fringe, my first solo-play and gave it a must-see review and then a list of improvements in the review that needed to be made (Honestly, the best and most constructive review ever!). That Must-See review helped Mark Makin make up his mind to really help me along, giving his time and booking me for performances with unsurpassed generosity, mentoring me in tour booking, forcing me to write out Arts Council application forms, publishing my first collection and generally aiming me towards artistic sustainability... something I've almost cracked. I met the other actor he was working with, the brilliant Gerard Logan, whose director, lovely Gareth Armstrong came on board to direct *"300 to 1"* and seriously upped my game. Thanks to the brilliant Peter Buckley Hill without whom not only would I have found it impossible to do Edinburgh financially (there's a reason why most of the breakthrough acts are predominantly white, male, middle-class... and fucking boring), but so many other Artists would too. Thanks to Fran and Norma, my lovely hosts who've saved me from sleeping the Edinburgh streets the last couple of years. There are so many others that I've met along this daisy chain, Fay Roberts whose support at a time of artistic fragility kept me going, Jackie Hagan for similar. Sophia Walker for allowing me to direct her first show *Around the World in 8 Mistakes*, an experience so rewarding, I've repeated it, and will do whenever asked. Thanks to Jillian and Rob, Erez and Shula, KL Thomas, Kenny and Julia for making New York as magical as New York can be, and it can be.

There have, as always with things like this, been so many others, without whom it wouldn't have happened in quite the way it has. I've not forgotten you, I love you, and thank you. I wanted to take this opportunity show you how organic the whole thing is, intrinsic, connected, magical, marvellous. Finally, thanks to Clive Birnie of Burning Eye without whom you wouldn't be holding this book, and finally, finally to you again, for holding it.

All best
MP
x